PENGUIN BOOKS

DATE			
SE 28 '97			
AP 11 '98			
DEC 10 01			
OCT 28 02			
DEC 05 02			
MAR 19 03			
JAN 2 04			
NOV 29 04			
AP 08 08			
NO 11 13			

BAKER & TAYLOR

WAR AND PEACE IN THE MIDDLE EAST

A CONCISE HISTORY
REVISED AND UPDATED

Avi Shlaim

PENGUIN BOOKS

To Tamar

PENGUIN BOOKS
Published by the Penguin Group
Penguin Books USA Inc., 375 Hudson Street,
New York, New York 10014, U.S.A.
Penguin Books Ltd, 27 Wrights Lane,
London W8 5TZ, England
Penguin Books Australia Ltd, Ringwood,
Victoria, Australia
Penguin Books Canada Ltd, 10 Alcorn Avenue,
Toronto, Ontario, Canada M4V 3B2
Penguin Books (N.Z.) Ltd, 182–190 Wairau Road,
Auckland 10, New Zealand

Penguin Books Ltd, Registered Offices:
Harmondsworth, Middlesex, England

First published in the United States of America by
Viking Penguin, a division of Penguin Books USA Inc., 1994
This revised and updated edition published in Penguin Books 1995

1 3 5 7 9 10 8 6 4 2

Published by arrangement with Whittle Communications L.P.

THE LIBRARY OF CONGRESS HAS CATALOGUED
THE HARDCOVER AS FOLLOWS:
War and peace in the Middle East:
a critique of American policy / Avi Shlaim.
p. cm.
ISBN 0-670-85330-5 (hc.)
ISBN 0 14 02.4564 2 (pbk.)
1. Middle East—Foreign relations. 2. Middle East—Foreign
relations—Europe. 3. Europe—Foreign relations—Middle East.
4. Middle East—Foreign relations—United States. 5. United
States—Foreign relations—Middle East. I. Title.
DS62.8.S53 1994
327.56—dc20 93-31015

Printed in the United States of America
Set in Sabon
Designed by Kathryn Parise
Maps by Ken Smith

C O N T E N T S

Introduction   1

1 The Post-Ottoman Syndrome   11

2 Succeeding John Bull   27

3 America Between Arabs and Israelis   37

4 Realpolitik in the Gulf   60

5 Tilting Toward Iraq   73

6 Desert Shield and Desert Storm   89

7 Madrid and After   104

8 Pax Americana   132

  Notes on Sources   147

WAR AND PEACE IN THE MIDDLE EAST

INTRODUCTION

Ever since Napoleon's expeditionary force landed in Egypt in 1798, the Middle East has been an object of rivalry among the great powers. The discovery of oil by the British in Persia in 1908 added even more to the region's strategic importance as the gateway between Europe and the Far East. In the aftermath of World War II, the Middle East became the principal source of energy for industrialized nations and an area of ever-growing importance for the global economy. At the same time, the Middle East was transformed into an arena of fierce competition between the two new superpowers, the Soviet Union and the United States. It became one of the major theaters of the Cold War between East and West.

Today, although the Cold War is over and although the Israel-PLO accord of September 13, 1993, marks the beginning of a new era in the century-old conflict between Jews and Arabs in Palestine, the Middle East remains one of the most

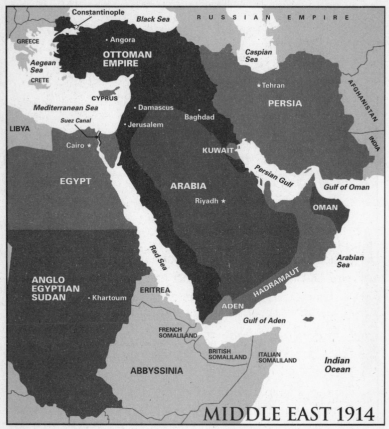

Although the Ottoman Empire once encompassed most of the Middle East, by 1914 more than two centuries of decline had greatly reduced its size.

volatile subsystems of the international political system. To the Western observer it frequently appears not simply unstable but irrational and unaccountably hostile, seething with political extremism and religious fanaticism. The politics of the region are indeed complex, but complexity should not be confused with irrationality. If we

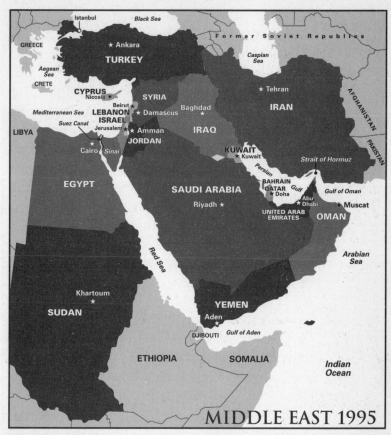

In 1995 Middle East boundaries remain largely as they were following the settlement between Britain and France that broke up the Ottoman Empire.

place the region's affairs in proper historical context, certain rules, patterns, and logic become apparent.

The key to the international politics of the Middle East lies in the relations between outside powers and local forces, whether governments, rulers, tribal chiefs, or warlords. In the nineteenth and early twentieth centuries, the club of great powers included the Ottoman Empire, the Austro-Hungarian Empire, czarist Russia, Germany, France, and Great Britain. Until the 1991 Gulf war, no one great power had controlled the Middle East in modern times. There had always been at least two great powers, and usually more than two, competing for control and influence. The potential for exploiting this competition was not lost on the local rulers. Some shrewdly assessed shifts in the balance of power, playing one great power off against another to advance local interests. It would be inaccurate, therefore, to think of the local powers as mere pawns in the game played by the great powers.

The involvement of the great powers is not a unique feature of the Middle East but one that affects, in varying degrees, all regions of the world. What distinguishes the Middle East is the intensity, pervasiveness, and profound impact of this involvement. No other part of the non-Western world has been so thoroughly and ceaselessly caught up in great-power politics. In his book *International Politics and the Middle East,* Princeton professor L. Carl Brown aptly describes the Middle East as "the most penetrated international relations subsystem in today's world."

Scholars disagree about the relative weights of external and internal forces in shaping the political evolution of the contemporary Middle East. The conventional view, popular among Middle Easterners and outsiders alike, is that external forces have played the decisive part. One critic of this view is Malcolm E. Yapp of the School of Oriental and African Studies of the University of London. In the introduction to his book *The Near East Since the First World War,* Professor Yapp notes that "the history of the modern Near East has often been written as though the states were driftwood in the sea of international affairs, their destinies shaped by the decisions of others." In considering the relations between international and regional powers, Professor Yapp concludes that "the dominant feature was the manipulation of the international powers by regional powers."

My own view is that the more conventional reading of Middle East history is rather simplistic: regional powers have enjoyed more leverage in dealing with outside powers than is generally recognized. Nevertheless, since this book is not about the internal political evolution of the Middle East but about the role of the Middle East in world politics, the emphasis is on the interests and policies of the great powers, especially the United States. External involvement in Middle East affairs in the twentieth century may be divided into four phases: the Ottoman, the European, the superpower, and the American.

The Ottoman phase provides the context for understanding the political culture of successor states. From 1516 to 1918, the Ottoman Turks ruled most of the Arab lands of the Middle East from Constantinople (now Istanbul). The sultans were all descendants of Osman, the Turkish founder of the Ottoman Empire. Their empire was dynastic, Islamic, and multiethnic. Within this ramshackle empire, the ethno-religious groups remained culturally autonomous; the Ottoman government respected and protected their distinctive laws and customs. The early Ottomans also rejected the Western notion of equality between sovereign states and instead divided the world into two spheres: *Dar al-Islam,* the abode of Islam where the laws of Islam prevailed, and *Dar al-Harb,* the abode of war where Muslims were enjoined to wage holy war, *jihad,* against infidels. The task of government was to enable the Islamic community to perform its duties to God. The distinction between church and state, central in Western political theory, was nonexistent.

Beginning in the late eighteenth century, the internal decline of the Ottoman Empire coincided with the expansion of European power. As a result of this shift in the balance of power, Islamic principles were adapted to European diplomatic conventions and practices, and eventually European ideas of how to organize international society prevailed. Yet the Ottoman legacy is important because so many of the statesmen, soldiers, and administrators of the successor states emerged from Ottoman political culture.

The Ottoman phase came to a close at the end of World War I. The European phase, during which Britain and France played the leading roles, lasted roughly from the end of World War I until the 1956 Suez crisis. During this period the colonial powers forged a new political and territorial order in the Middle East; they created states, drew their boundaries, and appointed their rulers.

British power expanded gradually, starting in the southeastern corner of the Arabian Peninsula. By 1882 Britain had occupied Egypt, where Ottoman rule had been unstable and indirect. Britain then conquered the Sudan and, by the early 1920s, had established itself in Palestine, Transjordan, and Iraq. Although France controlled Syria and Lebanon until 1946, Britain emerged as the dominant Western power. The inter-war period was, as Middle East specialist Elizabeth Monroe put it, Britain's moment in the Middle East. Throughout this period, Britain's chief interest was to shut out other great powers. The British made no systematic attempt to impregnate the states within their sphere of influence with British values or to impose the British model of parliamentary democracy.

The eclipse of European power in the Middle East came in the wake of the 1956 Suez war. Colonial rule, however, was not followed by superpower rule but by the rise to independence of the local states. The influence of the two new superpowers—the United States and the Soviet Union—was more limited than Britain's, and it exerted itself indirectly through alliances, economic assistance, and the supply of arms, not through direct political control or prolonged military occupation.

The superpower phase lasted from the mid-1950s until 1991, ending spectacularly with the collapse of the Soviet Union. The end of the Cold War left America dominant in world politics, and bipolarity made way for a unipolar international system in which America exercised global dominance. In the Middle East, as in other parts of the world, America no longer had to contend with Soviet rivalry. Within a remarkably short period, the Soviet Union was transformed from a powerful adversary into a junior partner.

Iraqi president Saddam Hussein was first to alert his fellow Arabs to the dangers inherent in the new situation. In a January 1990 speech, he predicted that the weakening of Moscow would allow America to become an unrivaled super-power in the Middle East. If Arabs were not vigilant, he warned, everything, including oil prices, would be ruled by the United States. Saddam failed to heed his own warning. By rolling Iraqi tanks into Kuwait on August 2, 1990, he sparked the first crisis of the post–Cold War order. America mobilized a vast international coalition, which included the Soviet Union, Britain, and France as junior partners. The coalition's purpose was to eject Iraq from Kuwait and restore the status quo.

Iraq was no match for America and its allies. The mother of all battles promised by Saddam ended in the mother of all military defeats for Iraq. America emerged as the unrivaled external power, holding sway over the entire region. President George Bush tried to present American hegemony as the foundation of collective security and the rule of law in international affairs. The Gulf war, he claimed, ushered in a New World Order. But Bush's claim exceeded the reality. The new order reflected the interests of the victors rather than any universal principles of justice or morality. Its hallmark, like that of the old order, was defense of the status quo.

America emerged as the principal guardian of Gulf security in the aftermath of the Gulf war. Having struggled against Western domination for most of the twentieth century, the Arab world was thrust back into a position of weakness, dependence, and subservience. The international politics of the Middle East had come full circle. A century that saw the rise and decline of Western rule in the Middle East ended with its reimposition. The collapse of the Ottoman Empire was followed by Britain's moment in the Middle East. The collapse of the Soviet Union, after a long interlude of Arab self-assertion and superpower rivalry, was followed by America's moment. The leading actors changed, but the old order survived. Far from creating a New World Order, America's victory in the Gulf war simply restored the old regional order in the Middle East.

C H A P T E R   1

THE POST-OTTOMAN
SYNDROME

The Ottoman Empire did not simply decline and disintegrate from within; it was destroyed from without. Its fate was sealed by its decision to enter World War I on the side of Germany. That decision, which erased any British motivation for preserving the empire, is the most significant in the history of the modern Middle East and the first move in its remaking: it led to the destruction of the Ottoman political order and to its replacement by a radically different order designed, imposed, and dominated by the victors.

During World War I the British made a number of promises in their search for allies against the Ottoman Empire. The three most important were to the French, the Arabs, and the Jews. First, in April 1916 Britain reached the secret Sykes-Picot Agreement with France, under which the two countries would divide the lands between the Mediterranean and the Persian Gulf into two "spheres of influence" in the event of victory. Second, Britain promised Hussein, the sharif of Mecca (great-grandfather of King Hussein of Jordan), that Britain would recognize and support Arab independence if Hussein took up arms against the Turks.

The third and most famous promise was the Balfour Declaration, a pledge made in November 1917 in a letter from British foreign secretary Arthur Balfour to Lord Rothschild, a leading British Zionist Jew. In it Balfour pledged Britain's support for a national home for the Jewish people in Palestine. Britain issued the Balfour Declaration in order to gain wartime support from Jews in Central Europe and the United States and in order to further its strategic interests in the Middle East. What the British failed to consider was the inevitability of a clash between Jewish and Arab nationalism.

Because of conflicting claims, dislodging the Turks from the Middle East proved easier than carving up their former territory. In the end, the League of Nations gave France the mandate over Syria and Lebanon, and Britain the mandate over Iraq, Transjordan, and Palestine.

The task of formulating a policy for dealing with the postwar challenge to Britain's position in the Middle East fell to Winston Churchill when he became colonial secretary in 1921. His principal adviser was Colonel T. E. Lawrence, better known as Lawrence of Arabia, a British officer sent to advise Sharif Hussein in the 1916 Arab revolt against the Turks. Under Lawrence's influence Churchill divided the British sphere into two states, to be headed by two of Hussein's sons, Faisal and Abdullah.

The throne of Iraq went to Faisal as a consolation prize for his eviction by the French from the throne of Syria. The British stage-managed his ascent in Baghdad, arranging a referendum that gave him a veneer of popular legitimacy (96 percent of Iraqis, they claimed, wanted him as their king). They also persuaded other candidates to withdraw (one was arrested and deported) and quelled the remaining opposition by force. Faisal ascended the throne on August 23, 1921.

As observed by Elie Kedourie, a critic of British policy and the author of *England and the Middle East,* the 1921 settlement had two notable results: first, it introduced anti-British sentiment as a fundamental principle of Iraqi politics, and second, "it justified and sanctioned violent and arbitrary proceedings and built them into the structure of Iraqi politics."

The delineation of Iraq's borders was equally arbitrary and equally calculated to suit Britain's own political, strategic, and commercial interests. The borders took no account of the aspiration of the Kurds to national self-determination or of the division of the rest of the population along religious lines into Sunni Muslims and Shiite Muslims. Originally two Ottoman provinces, Basra and Baghdad, composed Iraq. Later Britain added the oil-bearing province of Mosul in the north, dashing Kurdish hopes, raised by the 1920 Treaty of Sèvres, of an autonomous state. The treaty, in which the Allies outlined the division of the Ottoman Empire, had provided for the creation of an autonomous Kurdistan in western Anatolia and the province of Mosul. An unattributed quotation cited by journalists Pierre Salinger and Erik Laurent sums up the logic behind the enterprise: "Iraq was created by Churchill, who had the mad idea of joining two widely separated oil wells, Kirkuk and Mosul, by uniting three widely separated peoples: the Kurds, the Sunnis, and the Shiites."

The second stage in the creation of the British sphere was to give Faisal's elder brother, Abdullah, six months' probationary rule of the vacant lot that the British christened the Amirate of Transjordan (which gained independence in 1946 and was renamed the Hashemite Kingdom of Jordan in 1949). After six months, Britain issued a statement excluding Transjordan from the provisions for a Jewish National Home in the Palestine mandate. Churchill, well satisfied with his handiwork, frequently boasted that he had created the Amirate of Transjordan by the stroke of his pen one bright Sunday afternoon and still had time to paint the magnificent views of Jerusalem before sundown.

Britain's policy in Palestine provoked fierce Arab hostility. In 1920 Britain set up a civil administration headed by a high commissioner to govern the country directly, and the League of Nations incorporated into its mandate Balfour's promise to support a Jewish National Home. At the time of the Balfour Declaration, Jews constituted about 10 percent of Palestine's population. The British had acted on the assumption that the interests of Jews and Arabs could be reconciled, that the two races could live peacefully in a single state. But from the start a tragic contradiction was built into the Palestine mandate: Britain could meet its obligations to the Jews only at the expense of the Arab majority. Despite internal political divisions, the Palestine Arabs were united in their refusal to recognize the legality or authority of the British mandate and by their fear of Zionist intrusion. Their struggle was about self-preservation and self-determination.

Moreover, the enthusiasm with which Britain embraced the Zionist program in 1917 had largely evaporated by the early 1920s. The conflicting wartime promises, statements, and declarations made by the Allies regarding Palestine became a smoke screen of almost impenetrable density. One of the few honest remarks on the subject was made in retrospect by Balfour himself. "In short, so far as Palestine is concerned," he wrote, "the Powers have made no statement of fact which is not admittedly wrong, and no declaration of policy which, at least in the letter, they have not always intended to violate."

Britain emerged from World War I in a much stronger position to project its power from the coastline into the interior of the Arabian Peninsula, its traditional sphere of influence. Britain's policy was to reduce the friction between the rulers, to facilitate the use of traditional grazing grounds by

the local tribes, and to settle frontier disputes, thus
defining the jurisdictions of neighboring rulers. In
doing so Britain introduced European-type notions
of territorial sovereignty to an area where tribes
were much more important than the state, where
tribal borders were better understood than international ones, and where the law of the desert
prevailed.

During the 1922 negotiations to define the frontiers of Iraq, Kuwait, and the Najd (the forerunner
of present-day Saudi Arabia), Britain was capable
of acting in an arbitrary and autocratic manner to
further its political and strategic interests. The
British high commissioner for Iraq, Sir Percy Cox,
for instance, reprimanded Abd al-Aziz ibn al-
Rahman Al Faisal Al Saud, the mighty sultan of
Najd, as if he were a naughty schoolboy, reducing
him to tears. Britain forced Ibn Saud to yield land
to Iraq but later compensated him with two-thirds
of Kuwait's territory. Cox's borders also deliber-
ately restricted Iraq's access to the Persian Gulf.
The settlement satisfied none of the parties, least
of all Iraq, which felt entitled to Kuwait because
of former Ottoman boundaries. The introduction
of a European-style state system and international
relations thus produced mixed results: some disputes were settled, but others, like that between
Iraq and Kuwait, continued to generate friction
and instability.

The collapse of empires invariably has consequences for international order. The Ottoman Empire had provided a far from perfect political
system, but it worked. During World War I Britain

and its allies destroyed the old order in the Arabic-speaking Middle East without considering the long-term consequences. In the war's aftermath, they refashioned the Middle East in their own image, building a new political and territorial order on the ruins of the old. They created states, they nominated persons to govern them, and they laid down frontiers between them. But most of the new states were weak and unstable, the rulers lacked legitimacy, and the frontiers were arbitrary, illogical, and unjust, giving rise to powerful irredentist tendencies.

The new order had far-reaching consequences, settling Europe's century-long Eastern Question: who and what would succeed the Ottomans? But it also raised new questions: Would the people of the region accept a state system based on European ideas, interests, and management? Would they be willing to operate by the new ground rules? The answer is that powerful local forces, secular and religious, rejected both. Indeed, the absence of legitimacy, of a consensus on the rules of the political game, has been a central feature of Middle Eastern politics ever since.

To Arab nationalists the new order meant betrayal of wartime promises made by the Allies, military occupation, the division of the area into spheres of influence, and the exploitation of its raw materials. Planting what many saw as a dangerous imperialist bridgehead—the Jewish National Home—in Palestine further fueled hostility toward the authors of the new order.

In short, the postwar order imposed by Britain

and the Allies created a belt of turmoil and instability stretching from the Mediterranean to the Persian Gulf. The destruction of the Ottoman Empire was not followed by a new order but a new disorder—the post-Ottoman syndrome. Its consequences remain to the present day. In this sense the post–World War I peace settlement is not just a chapter in history but the essential background to contemporary politics. It lies at the root of the countless political clashes, territorial disputes, struggles for national liberation, and interstate wars that have become such familiar features of the politics of the Middle East. It lies at the heart of the current conflicts between the Arabs and Israel, between Arabs and other Arabs, between some Arabs and the West. As Field Marshal Earl Wavell, who served in the Palestine campaign, presciently observed, it was "a peace to end all peace."

The title of Elizabeth Monroe's book *Britain's Moment in the Middle East* encapsulates the interwar period. It was one of those rare moments in Middle Eastern history when the region was not an arena of competition or cooperation between world powers but of effective domination, or hegemony, by one of them. The Middle East's partial insulation from international affairs after World War I magnified the extent of this domination. Perhaps Britain enjoyed only the illusion of hegemony, but hegemony is a relative rather than an absolute term, and Britain was indisputably the dominant external power compared with all potential rivals.

The Ottoman Empire and the Austro-Hungarian Empire had both collapsed at the end of World War I. Russia, Britain's sparring partner in the nineteenth-century duel for Asian dominance, which one British officer dubbed "the Great Game," was hardly in a position to look beyond its southern borders in the aftermath of revolution and civil war. Fascist Italy was a rival in the Mediterranean but not a direct threat to Britain's position in the Middle East, and the threat from Nazi Germany became menacing only following the outbreak of World War II. Until then, France alone among the European powers was a serious rival to British predominance, but World War I had weakened France economically and the postwar settlement confined its diplomatic influence to Syria and Lebanon.

The United States, which had the capacity to challenge British hegemony and which most Middle Easterners preferred to either Britain or France, chose isolation. Britain wanted America to play a more active part, to share in the burden of sustaining the postwar settlement. "We cannot alone act as the policeman of the world," exclaimed British prime minister Andrew Bonar Law. President Warren Harding, however, declined to help. Nor did he share Woodrow Wilson's concern that the peoples of the Middle East be ruled by governments of their choosing. The principal object of his administration and those of his successors was to ensure the protection of America's private interests in the region: the educational and philanthropic activities of Protestant missionaries, trade relations, and the investments of American oil companies. These in-

terests could be protected, American leaders believed, without political and military commitments.
At the official level the Middle East remained a low
priority for the United States until the 1940s.

Here lay the principal difference between the
United States and Great Britain. Britain was an imperial power, and imperial preoccupations ranked
near the top of its foreign-policy priorities. The
United States was a world power with no imperial
preoccupations. It had no vital strategic interests,
no possessions, no military forces, no bases, no
mandates, and no clients in the region.

Yet the inter-war period was formative for the
United States in its dealings with both the Middle
East and Britain. Anglo-American relations were
remarkably cordial, because there was no serious
clash of interests and because State Department
officials deferred to their British colleagues' views.
The State Department had limited facilities for
training Arabists and a policy of rotating its officers
in the field. As a result American diplomats in Arab
capitals tended to reflect the insularity and inno-
cence of American society. The British could also be
insular, but they were not innocent. America was in
a sense Britain's pupil in the Middle East, and
American officials served their apprenticeship as the
understudies to Britain's distinguished Arabists. An
anecdote of the period describes a candidate for the
U.S. Foreign Service who, when asked what were
the most important things in the world, replied instantly, "Love and Anglo-American relations."

With such power, whether direct or indirect,
real or imagined, Britain exerted a profound effect.

During this formative period, the political and territorial shape of the modern Middle East did not evolve naturally, following its own internal laws, but was largely of British design, tailored to fit Britain's imperial needs. The worst blot on Britain's record and a major long-term source of strife and violence was the Palestine mandate. Separated from Transjordan in 1922, Palestine was governed by a succession of British high commissioners, all of whom tried and failed to reconcile the conflicting national aspirations of the Jewish and Arab populations.

In 1937 a Royal Commission headed by Earl Peel concluded that the mandate was unworkable. The recommendation of the six wise Englishmen was based on the principle that King Solomon had made famous: to partition the country between the two warring communities. From now on this was to be the basis of most international proposals for settling the Palestine problem. The Jews accepted the principle of partition and prepared to bargain over the details while the Palestine Arabs rejected the idea and reasserted their claim to the whole of the country.

It was during this period that the neighboring Arab states became directly involved in the Palestine conflict. The year 1936 had been a turning point; Palestine became a pan-Arab question, and the Arab states have remained involved ever since. The involvement of the Arab states did not facilitate the search for a solution, but it did induce Britain, which was increasingly preoccupied with the threat from Nazi Germany, to shift toward appeasement of the Palestine Arabs. The partition plan was abandoned. In May 1939 Britain issued a White Paper, which came close to repudiating the Balfour Declaration by placing strict limits on Jewish immigration and land purchases and accepting the Arab claim to self-determination.

Declining support from Britain and persistent rejection of their national claims by the local Arabs led Jewish leaders to seek an understanding with the rulers of neighboring Arab states. Their one great success was with their neighbor to the east. On November 17, 1947, Golda Meir reached a secret agreement with King Abdullah of Transjordan: after Britain's withdrawal, Palestine would be divided between the Jewish Agency—the Zionist organization authorized to develop a national homeland—and Transjordan. But on November 29, 1947, the United Nations passed a historic resolution, partitioning Palestine into two independent states, one Jewish and one Arab. The Jews accepted the resolution, and when the British mandate reached its inglorious end at midnight on May 14, 1948, they proclaimed their own state: Israel. The Arab states rejected the UN resolution and sent their armies to do battle with the infant state. The first Arab-Israeli war quickly developed into a land grab. The winners were the Israelis, who extended their borders beyond the UN lines, and Abdullah, who captured the West Bank and later annexed it to Transjordan. The losers were the Palestinians, who have been without a homeland ever since.

A climactic year in Middle Eastern history was

Left: The 1947 United Nations partition plan proposed a patchwork of Arab and Jewish areas, with Jerusalem to be placed under UN auspices. Right: By the 1949 Arab-Israeli armistice, Israel had extended its borders to include most of Palestine.

1948. It witnessed the spectacular emergence of a Jewish state after two thousand years of exile and the humiliating defeat of the Arab armies at the hands of this state. It was a year of Jewish triumph and Palestinian tragedy.

The State of Israel made its entrance into history in a war against the Arabs. For the Israelis it was a war of survival. There can be no doubt that the Arabs would have destroyed the Israeli intruders had they had the power. This knowledge reinforced the Zionist conviction, as natural to the hawks as it was unpalatable to the doves, that a state created by the sword would have to live by the sword.

23

As the moderate American-Zionist leader Nahum Goldmann notes in his autobiography, the military victory of 1948 had a marked psychological effect on Israel:

> It seemed to show the advantages of direct action over negotiation and diplomacy. The victory offered such a glorious contrast to the centuries of persecution and humiliation, of adaptation and compromise, that it seemed to indicate the only direction that could possibly be taken from then on. To brook nothing, tolerate no attack, cut through Gordian knots, and shape history by creating facts seemed so simple, so compelling, so satisfying that it became Israel's policy in its conflict with the Arab world.

The year 1948 had similarly profound psychological and political consequences for the Arabs. In Arabic, 1948 is called *al-nakba,* the catastrophe. For the Palestinians 1948 did mark the most catastrophic defeat in their protracted fight against the Jewish National Home. In 1917 some 690,000 Palestinians (compared to 85,000 Jews) formed a community that controlled nearly all of Palestine. By 1948 they had become an impotent minority inside a Jewish state. Some 700,000 Palestinians became refugees. The trauma of defeat, dispersal, and exile seared itself into their collective memory. They resolved to return to liberate Palestine.

A series of coups, revolutions, and political convulsions in the catastrophe's aftermath gripped the Arab world. Those rulers and regimes held responsible did not survive long. Colonel Husni Zaim, the Syrian chief of staff, staged a coup d'état in March 1949, setting a pattern of military intervention in politics. In July 1951 King Abdullah of Transjordan was assassinated by a Palestinian nationalist in Jerusalem. In July 1952 a group of Free Officers—young nationalist officers of the Egyptian army led by Gamal Abdul Nasser, who had served as a brigade major in the Palestine war— overthrew the Egyptian monarchy.

The loss of Palestine also colored Arab attitudes toward the Western powers. Many Arabs still view Israel as a bridgehead planted in their midst by Western powers determined to keep Arabs divided and to frustrate their national ambitions. As the power that issued the Balfour Declaration, Britain bears the brunt of these accusations despite its repeated claim that support for a Jewish National Home in Palestine did not imply support for turning Palestine into a Jewish state. In fact, the one thing Britain did not do during the twilight of its rule in Palestine was act as midwife in the birth of Israel. Britain simply accepted the emergence as inevitable. If Britain was guilty of anything, it was of helping King Abdullah frustrate the establishment of a Palestinian state.

America played a marginal role in the birth of Israel. It lobbied for the UN partition plan and it was the first to extend diplomatic recognition to the newborn state. In 1948 it indirectly helped the Israelis by insisting on an embargo of arms into Palestine. And President Truman supported Israel's claim to the Negev, the desert area in the south where a number of Jewish settlements had been established. Yet the Arabs persist in seeing America as Israel's co-sponsor, and this perception is the source of a deep and abiding hostility and mistrust.

In his 1986 book *They Say the Lion,* Sir Anthony Parsons, a British diplomat who spent much of his career in the Arab world, singles out the Palestine problem as the most enduring and terrible part of Britain's legacy in the Middle East:

> Palestine has become the cardinal point of reference for the domestic politics of Arab states, for the relationship between member states of the Arab League, for the conduct of Arab diplomacy with the outside world. . . . For nearly 40 years Palestine has dominated the agenda of the United Nations. . . . Palestine has, in a nutshell, become one of the most pervasive and dramatic of global problems since the end of the Second World War. Strange to think that it all began with a short, one-sentence letter from the British foreign secretary to Lord Rothschild in November 1917.

After the British mandate over Palestine expired and the State of Israel was established, the international politics of the Middle East could be reduced to three essential dimensions: the Arab-Israeli conflict, inter-Arab relations, and great power involvement in the affairs of the region. The Palestine problem lay at the core of the Arab-Israeli conflict. Both regional and international politics continued to revolve, to a remarkable degree, around this problem.

CHAPTER 2

SUCCEEDING
JOHN BULL

After World War II the United States had only a
peripheral interest in the Middle East and had
little desire to take Britain's place as the region's
self-appointed protector. Congressman Emmanuel
Celler of New York reflected the popular anti-
imperialist stance best when he said that the trouble with postwar Britain was "too damned much
socialism at home and too much damned imperialism abroad." There was a widely held belief that
granting the Arab countries independence would
ensure their support in the emerging Cold War with
the Soviet Union. The same ideology inclined
America to sympathize with the Free Officers who,
led by future president Gamal Abdul Nasser, carried out the 1952 Egyptian revolution against the
established regime. The United States saw them as
a progressive force whose introduction of social

and economic reforms would help curb the appeal of communism in the Middle East.

With the onset of the Cold War, the overriding need to contain Soviet expansion dwarfed Anglo-American differences about Arab nationalism. Britain initiated a number of schemes for the defense of the Middle East, culminating in the 1955 Baghdad Pact, a regional alliance including Iraq, Turkey, Iran, and Pakistan. The United States encouraged and helped finance the pact but did not become a member.

To the Arab states, the Israeli threat was much more real than that from the Soviet Union, and, with the exception of Iraq, they refused to join the pact. Nasser denounced it as an attempt to perpetuate Western domination. The Arab refusal led U.S. secretary of state John Foster Dulles to concentrate on building a "northern tier" of the states bordering the Soviet Union—Turkey, Iran, and Afghanistan—as a barrier to Soviet advances. American-Egyptian relations were further strained by Egypt's nonalignment in the Cold War. When America refused Nasser's request for arms, he turned to the Soviet Union, a move resulting in the September 1955 arms deal with Czechoslovakia. The supply of arms, including Soviet aircraft and tanks, enabled the Soviet Union to leapfrog over the northern tier and establish itself in the heartland of the Middle East.

Relations between Egypt and the West deteriorated further when America withdrew its offer to finance the Aswan Dam, a project crucial to Egypt's economic development, promising both electric power and a means of irrigating large land areas. Nasser retaliated on July 26, 1956, the fourth anniversary of the Egyptian revolution, by announcing the nationalization of the Suez Canal—a potent symbol of colonial domination. Although not illegal, this action convinced prime minister Anthony Eden that Britain and its allies would have to force Nasser from power. Much of Britain's oil imports passed through the canal, and Eden was adamant that Nasser must not be permitted to "have his hand on our windpipe." Because Dwight Eisenhower was equally convinced that force should not be used, Eden resorted to the famous collusion with the Israelis and the French, paving the way for the tripartite attack on Egypt in October 1956. Although each of the countries had its own motives, the aim that united them was to bring about Nasser's downfall. The three planned an Israeli invasion of the Sinai. France and Britain then demanded that both Egypt and Israel withdraw ten miles from the Suez Canal. When Nasser refused, France and Britain attacked Egypt.

Britain was thus doubly guilty: guilty of aggression against Egypt and guilty of calculated deceit against its great ally. "It [was] rather fun to be at Number 10 the night we smashed the Anglo-American alliance" was how one official from the Foreign Office put it. Eisenhower was furious that his persistent warnings against the use of force had gone unheeded. He certainly did not lie still, as Harold Macmillan, the hawkish chancellor of the exchequer, had predicted. In fact, Eisenhower led the pack in the UN General Assembly that hounded

Britain to end the attack. By putting pressure on the pound sterling and threatening Britain with oil sanctions, Eisenhower swiftly ended Eden's war—and shortly afterward his premiership. Eden, wrote the *Sunday Times* on January 16, 1977, "was the last prime minister to believe Britain was a great power and the first to confront a crisis which proved beyond doubt that she was not."

Suez was a watershed in Britain's decline not only in the Middle East but worldwide. The expedition's intention was to show that Britain was still a lion and that any local monkey that twisted its tail would not go unpunished. But as CIA official Chester L. Cooper put it, Suez turned out to be "the lion's last roar." On the road to Suez, Britain's leaders managed to combine immorality (disregard for international law), political folly (collusion with the Israelis), and incompetence (failed execution of the military operation). Suez was the wrong war, at the wrong time, on the wrong issue, against the wrong enemy. Nasser's anti-imperialism represented the wave of the future in the Arab world, and Britain tried to turn it back. Although some argue that Britain was bound to make a last stand against imperial decline, it could have bowed to the inevitable with more grace, as the Labor government had done over India.

While Britain's prestige plummeted, Nasser's soared. Far from being toppled, he emerged the hero of the newly independent Arab world. Arabs viewed the Suez affair as a colonial rearguard action that, thanks to the Egyptian leader's courage and determination, ended in Britain's ignominious withdrawal. The regimes friendly to Britain were shaken to their foundations, as was the special relationship between Britain and America.

Suez was thus an event of worldwide consequence, a watershed not just for Britain but for the postwar world in general. It was the last occasion when the European powers tried to impose their will on the region by force. In the aftermath of Suez, the European phase in the history of the Middle East gave way to the superpower phase: the limited rivalry between Britain and France was replaced by the global rivalry and conflicting ideologies of the United States and the Soviet Union. The Middle East became another theater in the Cold War.

Fearing that the Soviet Union would try to fill the power vacuum created by the eclipse of Britain and France, on March 9, 1957, the United States announced the ill-fated Eisenhower Doctrine. The doctrine offered U.S. military and economic aid to any Middle Eastern state threatened by international communism, mistakenly assuming that the local powers also looked at Middle East politics in terms of superpower rivalry. In fact, the Arab states were much more preoccupied with their own rivalries and with Israel than with the Soviet threat. In the Middle East, as in Korea and Indochina, the force of indigenous nationalism could help quell the spread of communism. But by identifying the radical Arab regimes with international communism, the Eisenhower Doctrine instead pushed them into the arms of the Soviet Union.

Conversely, the doctrine added a reason for countries threatened by these regimes, notably Israel, to portray themselves as allies of the West in the struggle against communism.

The Eisenhower Doctrine exemplifies the tendency that became the bane of American Middle Eastern policy: seeing the region through the distorting prism of the Cold War. It helped turn the Middle East into a jousting ground for the superpowers and international politics into a zero-sum game in which one player's gain was seen as the other's loss. The region's home-grown conflicts, bitter enough on their own, became virtually insoluble with the involvement of fiercely competitive outside powers.

The 1958 civil war in Lebanon between Lebanese and Arab nationalists was the first clear manifestation of the new pattern of international politics in the era of the superpowers and bipolarity. The crisis in Lebanon was precipitated by the Iraqi revolution of July 14, 1958. It originated in a domestic power struggle between Arab radicals and Arab conservatives; it was not instigated by the Soviet Union. In American minds, however, it raised the specter of Soviet dominion. In Iraq, an army-led revolution brutally overthrew the pro-British monarchy. By failing to break with Britain for its collusion with Israel against Egypt, the Baghdad regime had been fatally compromised. It was not the Soviet Union but Britain's own folly that served as the real catalyst in the Iraqi revolution.

The revolution further weakened Britain's position in the Middle East. In the first place, revolutionary Iraq's defection from the British-sponsored Baghdad Pact emasculated the organization. Second, ever since Churchill's days as colonial secretary, Britain's position had rested on two main pillars: the Hashemite regime in Baghdad and the Hashemite regime in Amman, Jordan. The destruction of the Iraqi branch of the Hashemite family left Jordan's King Hussein wobbling on his throne. He appealed for help, and in response British paratroops flew to Jordan to prevent a repetition of the events in Baghdad. When the danger passed, the paratroops quietly returned home.

The third and concurrent crisis plunged Lebanon into civil war. Camille Chamoun, the beleaguered pro-Western president of Lebanon, invoked the Eisenhower Doctrine although he faced no threat from international communism. In response, American Marines landed on the Beirut beaches. The emergence of a compromise candidate ended the civil war, and the Marines withdrew. America's first military intervention in the Middle East thus paradoxically resulted in the replacement of Chamoun's extremely pro-American government by a neutral one headed by General Fuad Chehab. Yet the Eisenhower administration persisted in seeing the events that unfolded in Lebanon as an international crisis rather than a local one and in claiming that it had scored a victory in the power struggle against Moscow.

Despite the Suez fiasco and its political fallout in Arab countries to the north, Britain maintained its semicolonial position east of Suez for another decade, until financial pressures forced its withdrawal. Ousted from Egypt, Britain nevertheless remained popular with the rulers of Arabia, who needed its help in dealing with internal subversion, in settling local disputes, and in fending off the territorial claims of powerful neighbors. Britain's quasi-imperial role was an anachronism in a world in which anti-imperialism, decolonization, and nonalignment had become guiding beacons. The rulers themselves, however, were not ready to stand on their own and did not press to swap British protection for independence. Britain, for its part, needed the status quo in the Gulf to maintain the free flow of cheap crude oil and protect the investments of its oil companies, whose revenue was critical to its economy.

The risks involved in British withdrawal became apparent in 1961 when Britain granted independence to Kuwait. The republican regime in Baghdad under General Abd al-Karim Qasim revived the long-standing Iraqi claim to Kuwait, whose ruler sought and obtained British protection. With the United States' help, Britain immediately airlifted 6,000 troops in anticipation of invasion. Two months later the troops left, replaced by an all-Arab force sent by the Arab League, an organization founded in 1945 to promote cooperation among the Arab states of the Middle East. British military intervention and strong support from the Arab League enabled Kuwait to preserve its newly won independence against the Iraqi challenge.

The Labor Party, which came to power in 1964, continued Britain's traditional policy. Harold Wilson and his colleagues considered their country a world power, and they were committed to maintaining a military presence east of Suez. But the difficulty of sustaining commitments without the Suez base, increasing political pressure at home, and acute financial crisis led to Britain's January 1968 announcement that its military presence in the Persian Gulf would end by the close of 1971.

At the time of the announcement, the British presence involved about 6,000 ground troops, as well as naval and air support units, costing around £12 million a year (about $29 million at the exchange rate of the time). The rulers of the Persian Gulf received the British announcement with dismay and offered to meet Britain's expenses out of their mounting oil revenues. Defense secretary Denis Healey poured scorn on the suggestion that the British become "mercenaries for people who like to have British troops around," and the Labor government considered it politically unwise to maintain its military presence east of Suez. It signaled its retreat from empire by applying for membership in the European Economic Community.

Once the decision to withdraw had been made, the question remained how to terminate the protective treaties between Britain and its allies—some of which had been in force for a century and a half—without precipitating chaos and instability. Withdrawal from a region that supplied 32 percent of the world's petroleum and contained 58 percent of the proven oil reserves was potentially worrisome. But the process was carried out smoothly and amicably. Mohammad Reza Pahlavi, the shah of Iran,

who had long claimed the oil-rich islands of
Bahrain as the fourteenth province of his empire,
abandoned the claim and came forward instead to
claim the role of policeman of the Persian Gulf.
A major challenger to the status quo thus became
its defender, earning the gratitude of the Western
powers.

Withdrawal from the Persian Gulf symbolized
the end of Pax Britannica, and, for the region, the
relatively stable period of British dominance. It
also meant the end of a security system that had
operated in Arabia since the first half of the nineteenth century. Britain's role as the manager of
Gulf security had had three aspects: insulating the
region from penetration by other great powers,
preventing interstate conflicts such as those between Iraq and Kuwait, and helping local rulers
foil military coups and combat subversion. The secret of Britain's success lay in keeping a low profile
and a small military presence and, above all, in
limiting the supply of arms. This secret was forgotten in the post-imperial era, when Uncle Sam succeeded John Bull as the area's preeminent Western
power and the manager of Gulf security.

C H A P T E R 3

AMERICA BETWEEN
ARABS AND ISRAELIS

One of the principal legacies of European domination of the Middle East is borders arbitrarily imposed and therefore disputed and unstable. Of the
various territorial quarrels, that between Arabs and
Israelis is the most prominent, bitter, and protracted. Six Arab-Israeli wars punctuate postwar
Middle East history: the 1948 Palestine war, the
1956 Suez war, the June 1967 Six-Day War, the
1969–70 War of Attrition, the October 1973 Yom
Kippur War, and the 1982 Lebanon war. America
remained on the sidelines in 1948, and in 1957
compelled Israel to return the Sinai Peninsula to
Egypt. With each successive war, however, America
became more deeply committed to Israel, culminating in direct military involvement following Israel's
1982 invasion of Lebanon.

During the era of superpower domination, the

Middle East became one of the world's most keenly contested regions. Because it adjoined the Soviet Union's southern border, it was vitally important to Soviet security. On the American scale of world priorities, the Middle East came second, after Europe. With the 1955 Czech arms deal, which thinly disguised the supply of Soviet weapons to Egypt, the Cold War arrived in the Middle East. Until its end the region remained an arena of superpower competition for influence, strategic advantage, and access to oil. During this period America's Middle East policy was largely an extension of its Cold War strategy.

One of the distinguishing characteristics of a superpower is that its outlook and influence are global rather than regional. But the United States had four basic interests that made the Middle East an area of special importance and special responsibility: first, the interest during the Cold War in containing Soviet influence and expansion; second, and of growing importance since the 1973–74 oil crisis, the need to preserve Western access to two-thirds of the world's known petroleum reserves; third, the interest in curbing Arab radicalism and in sustaining the conservative, pro-Western regimes in the area; and last but not least, the long-standing and deeply felt commitment to the security and well-being of Israel.

Policy makers found it difficult to devise a Middle East policy that would serve the full range of America's interests. Indeed, the attempt to devise such a policy was an attempt to square a circle. Since the first three interests were not only compatible but mutually reinforcing, devising a strategy for furthering them all simultaneously was not difficult. But the commitment to Israel would not fit easily into an overall framework. Much of the debate on American policy was fundamentally about how the fourth interest related to the first three. As Jimmy Carter observed, "The simple truth is that one of the most cherished, complicated, frustrating, challenging, and least understood of our nation's relationships is with Israel."

Two schools of thought on America's relations with the Middle East emerged in the 1960s: the globalist and the regionalist. The debate was between those who looked at the region through the prism of the Cold War and the global struggle for power between East and West, and those who looked at it in terms of its own problems and the American stake in solving them. The globalists, or Cold Warriors, focused on the Soviet Union as a strategic rival and on the post-colonial Third World as a power vacuum that the Soviet Union was bound to try to fill. Thus, their overriding aim was to preempt the Soviet Union and its clients. The regionalists focused less on the Soviet Union than on the local sources of conflict. Their aim was to win friends and promote stability by helping the local actors solve their problems.

The State of Israel remained a major bone of contention in the doctrinal debate between globalists and regionalists. Militarily, politically, and morally, the globalists viewed Israel as an asset, a bulwark against Soviet penetration and a bastion of regional order. The regionalists viewed Israel as a liability. Israel, they argued, opens the door to Soviet penetration on the side of the Arabs and, conversely, prevents America from developing a positive relationship with Arab societies and their regimes.

The globalist-regionalist debate translated into two very different policies toward the Arab-Israeli conflict. The globalists advocated what might be termed an "Israel-first" policy, whereas the regionalists advocated a more evenhanded approach. According to the proponents of the Israel-first policy, the conflict stemmed from the peculiar psychological hang-ups of the Arabs. They perceived the Arab world as so backward, so seething with hostility, and so endemically volatile that it precluded a durable peace. Israel, they felt, was America's only advanced, intelligent, and reliable ally in the area. Under these circumstances, America's best bet was to maintain Israel's superiority over its adversaries through regular infusions of money and arms; these would enable it not only to deal with threats to its security, but also to fend off challenges to American interests from radical, Islamic, and Soviet-backed forces. Complaints from Arab quarters about America's partiality toward Israel were of no practical consequence, said the globalists, since the Arabs needed America more than America needed them.

Proponents of the evenhanded approach retorted that uncritical support for Israel undermined America's interests in the Arab Middle East and the Islamic world. It drove the radical regimes into the arms of Moscow, placed great strain on the pro-Western regimes, and fed the growth of radical Islamic fundamentalist movements. Israel's occupation of Arab land and refusal to recognize the national rights of the Palestinians were, according to this view, the fundamental problems. America's best hope of bringing stability to the region as well as safeguarding its own interests lay in the pursuit of an Arab-Israeli settlement and, above all, a settlement of the Palestinian problem.

The Six-Day War of 1967, also known as the June war, was a turning point for America, as it was for all participants in the Arab-Israeli conflict. Since 1967 the Israel-first school has dominated American policy. But this school did not win simply on the merit of its arguments. Domestic politics played a crucial part in settling the argument in favor of Israel's supporters. Of course, domestic politics influence the making of foreign policy in all countries; in America, however, this is especially true on issues involving Israel.

The special relationship between America and Israel rests on a foundation of cultural affinity and common values. Many Americans, both Jew and Gentile, admire Israel's pioneering spirit, its social and economic achievements, its settlement of the land, its courage, and its democratic ways in a region inhospitable to democracy. Israel stands for and defends itself in the name of ideals with which Americans readily identify.

A more concrete factor behind American support is the power of the American Israel Public Affairs Committee (AIPAC), popularly known as the Jewish lobby—one of the most powerful lobbies in

American politics. Of the institutions involved in the formulation and conduct of American Middle East policy, Congress is the most susceptible to AIPAC's influence, whereas the State Department is the least susceptible. But the president holds the key; he bears ultimate responsibility for Middle East policy and arbitrates when conflicts arise between Congress and other agencies. American policy can therefore best be understood by examining the ideas, attitudes, and preferences of the men at the top—the president and his White House advisers.

President Truman was a fervent supporter of Israel due partly to his Cold War outlook but largely to domestic political considerations. President Eisenhower regarded Israel as a hindrance to America's global policy for the containment of communism and to its regional strategy for the settlement of the Arab-Israeli conflict. President Kennedy moved toward a more evenhanded approach. He accepted Israel as a positive force, consistent with American ideals, but he also cultivated links with the Arab world's nationalist and radical leaders, notably Egyptian president Gamal Abdul Nasser. Under President Johnson, America moved closer to an informal alliance with Israel and the more conservative forces in the Arab world, and away from Nasser and the nationalists.

The Six-Day War resulted from brinkmanship by Nasser that went over the brink. Israel not only won a spectacular military victory, but also captured the Sinai Peninsula from Egypt, the West Bank from Jordan, and the Golan Heights from

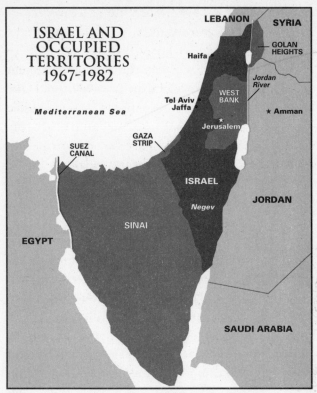

ISRAEL AND
OCCUPIED
TERRITORIES
1967-1982

In the Six-Day War of 1967, Israel captured the Sinai Peninsula and the Gaza Strip from Egypt, the West Bank from Jordan, and the Golan Heights from Syria.

Syria. (See map, above.) Believing Eisenhower had made a mistake in letting Nasser off the hook during the Suez crisis, Johnson insisted that the Egyptian president demonstrate a commitment to peace before he would exert pressure on Israel to withdraw from the newly occupied territories. He also enunciated the five principles on which peace should be based: the recognized right of national life, justice for the refugees, innocent maritime passage, limits on the arms race, and political independence and territorial integrity for all.

Despite its support for Israel, America did not share the Israeli interpretation of Security Council Resolution 242 of November 22, 1967, which remains the basis of all international efforts to settle the Arab-Israeli conflict. Its preamble stresses "the inadmissibility of the acquisition of territory by war and the need to work for a just and lasting peace." The resolution called on Israel to withdraw its armed forces "from territories occupied in the recent conflict" and on the Arabs to end their belligerency and respect Israel's right to live peacefully within secure and recognized boundaries. The resolution was ambiguous in referring to "territories" rather than "the territories." According to the Arab interpretation, 242 called for an immediate withdrawal from all occupied territories. To the Israelis it meant direct negotiations between the parties, leading to the conclusion of formal peace treaties that embodied secure and recognized boundaries. This allowed for a substantial redrawing of the map. The American interpretation contemplated minor adjustments in the western frontier of the West Bank, demilitarization measures in the Sinai and the Golan Heights, and a fresh look at the status of Jerusalem—not the retention of substantial tracts of Arab land in Israeli hands. Three years of intensive international diplomacy failed to reconcile the conflicting interpretations, and the territorial status quo gradually hardened.

Global strategy dictated the policy of President

Nixon and national security adviser Henry Kissinger toward the conflict. Their aim, as Kissinger once revealed in a private briefing, was to expel the Soviets from the Middle East. Israel held a special place in the 1969 Nixon Doctrine designed to protect American interests in the Third World not by committing American troops as in Vietnam but by backing local allies. In line with this, America offered Israel diplomatic support, economic assistance, and arms on an ever-growing scale.

The military prowess Israel demonstrated in the Six-Day War helped transform the unequal U.S.-Israel relationship into a strategic partnership. Israel's ability to use force in such a crushing and decisive manner provided a sharp contrast to the impotence of American forces in Vietnam. Having such a virile proxy in the Middle East enticed Nixon and Kissinger to assume military risks polar to Soviet caution.

In 1969 Nasser, frustrated by the standstill on the diplomatic front, began the War of Attrition, a series of artillery duels across the Suez Canal intended to dislodge Israel from the Sinai. In January 1970, at the war's height, Israel decided to raise the stakes. Reports from ambassador Yitzhak Rabin of private discussions with Nixon and Kissinger persuaded the Israeli cabinet to begin bombing Egypt, with the primary aim of toppling Nasser. Instead the raids fostered a mood of militant defiance in Egypt and brought in the Soviets, whose involvement the Americans could hardly have welcomed.

In September 1970 Israel deterred Syrian intervention on the side of Palestinian guerrillas against

Jordan's King Hussein. This local crisis, which Nixon and Kissinger mistook for a Soviet-inspired challenge to the pro-American monarchy, brought about a fundamental reorientation of American policy. It was a classic failure of globalists, obsessed with the Soviet threat, to understand the region's political dynamics. Nixon and Kissinger concluded that the American-Israeli partnership was the key to combating Soviet influence in the Middle East and to maintaining regional stability. The thrust of American policy from then on was to maintain the territorial status quo; international efforts aimed at a negotiated settlement of Arab-Israeli differences became secondary. America viewed military balance, or rather Israeli superiority, as the key to stability and eventual peace on Israel's terms.

Nasser died in September 1970, exhausted by his efforts to mediate between King Hussein and the Palestinian guerrillas. He was succeeded by Anwar el-Sadat, who switched almost immediately from a policy of military confrontation with Israel to one of negotiation. In February 1971 UN mediator Gunnar Jarring sent identical questionnaires to Egypt and Israel in an attempt to break the deadlock over Resolution 242. Sadat gave all the commitments Jarring asked for, but Israel stated flatly that it would not return to the lines of June 4, 1967.

Sadat then came up with his own diplomatic initiative. He offered Israel an interim settlement based on a limited Israeli withdrawal into Sinai and the reopening of the Suez Canal. Golda Meir,

who more than any other Israeli leader personified
its policy of immobilism, rejected Sadat's terms.
Nixon and Kissinger condoned Israel's diplomatic
intransigence and thus became accomplices in
blocking peace negotiations. The joint Israeli-
American policy was to let Sadat sweat it out, his
range of options constantly narrowing, until he
had little choice but to sue for peace on Israel's
terms. Instead Sadat chose to fight. On Yom Kippur, October 6, 1973, Egypt and Syria launched a
surprise attack on Israel. This attack broke the
diplomatic stalemate and provoked superpower
intervention.

To blame the Soviet Union for frustrating a settlement of the Arab-Israeli conflict in the six years
between the Six-Day War and the Yom Kippur
War is to twist the facts. Although the Soviet
Union was allied to the Arab radical regimes, it
never questioned Israel's right to exist and indeed
offered to guarantee Israel within the pre-1967
borders. Like America, the Soviet Union took Resolution 242 to mean an Israeli withdrawal to the
old borders with only minor modifications. Unlike
America, the Soviet Union strictly rationed the
supply of arms to its allies in the region. In fact,
the Soviets' refusal to give Egypt a military option
against Israel led Sadat to expel all Soviet advisers
in 1972. All the available evidence suggests that
following Sadat's rise to power there was opportunity for a negotiated settlement. The chance was
missed not because of the Soviet stand but as a result of Israeli intransigence backed by global
strategists in the White House.

The Yom Kippur War shattered the two major assumptions underlying the Nixon-Kissinger policy: that a strong Israel would deter the Arabs from going to war and that the territorial status quo could be maintained indefinitely in Israel's favor. While the war was in progress, Kissinger began to develop a policy that for the first time had a significant Arab component. It committed America to a more evenhanded approach and to a step-by-step diplomatic process. The first step was the disengagement agreements between Israel and Egypt and then Israel and Syria brokered by Kissinger in 1974. The former divided the area between the Suez Canal and the Giddi and Mitla passes in Sinai into Egyptian and Israeli zones separated by a UN buffer zone. The latter called for Israeli withdrawal from Syrian territory east of the Golan Heights and established a second buffer zone.

The next step was a second Sinai disengagement agreement, or Sinai II. The 1975 agreement established America as its guarantor and committed Israel to pulling out of the Giddi and Mitla passes and to relinquishing Sinai oil fields. In return for Israeli cooperation, the United States promised military assistance, oil supplies, and economic aid. Some observers considered the commitments out of proportion with Israel's sacrifices. George Ball, an undersecretary of state in the Kennedy and Johnson administrations and a leading advocate of the regionalist approach, claimed Sinai II "amounted to a vast real estate deal in which the United States bought a slice of the Sinai Desert from Israel for a

huge financial and political consideration and then
paid Egypt for accepting it."

Under Sadat's leadership, Egypt moved from
the Soviet to the American camp. Sadat viewed
America as the only power capable of delivering
territorial concessions from the Israelis. He once
remarked that America held 99 percent of the
cards in the Middle East. In November 1977 Sadat
embarked on his dramatic visit to Jerusalem. By
this time Democrat Jimmy Carter was president.
The moderate Labor Party, which had ruled Israel
since 1948, had lost power to the right-wing Likud
Party, headed by Menachem Begin. The Labor
Party's foreign policy was dictated primarily by
security considerations, the Likud's by ideology.
Whereas the Labor Party denied any national
rights to the Palestinians and favored territorial
compromise with Jordan over the West Bank, the
Likud Party viewed Jordan as a Palestinian state
and the West Bank as an inalienable part of Israel.
It was entirely consistent with this ideology for the
Likud to give back Sinai in return for peace with
Egypt and yet to refuse to withdraw from the West
Bank.

Carter's election had promised a fresh approach
to the Arab-Israeli conflict, a change from the
globalism of the Nixon-Kissinger era to the regionalism advocated by George Ball. Carter and his advisers agreed with Ball about the need to move
from Kissinger's step-by-step approach toward a
comprehensive settlement of the Arab-Israeli dispute, including a solution to the Palestinian problem. They began to work toward a conference in

Geneva at which the Soviet Union and all parties to the dispute would be represented. But following Sadat's announcement of a trip to Jerusalem, where he would address the Israeli Knesset, Carter had little choice but to abandon his Geneva plan in favor of a separate Egyptian-Israeli accord.

In September 1978 Carter invited Sadat and Begin—two "unguided missiles," as one State Department official described them—to the presidential retreat at Camp David. After thirteen days of tough and often stormy negotiations, the three heads of state emerged to sign two agreements: "a framework for peace in the Middle East," which dealt with the Palestinian problem, and "a framework for peace between Israel and Egypt."

The second of these was a straightforward application of the "land for peace" principle. It provided for the restoration of Sinai to Egyptian sovereignty and the normalization of relations between Israel and Egypt.

The attempt to deal with the Palestinian problem, however, was anything but straightforward. It provided for a five-year transition period after the election of a self-governing authority and "full autonomy" to the inhabitants of the West Bank and Gaza. Negotiations about the final status of the territories were to be held before the end of the transition period, although it was unclear who would represent the Palestinians. The absence of a firm link between the two agreements aroused Arab suspicions that Begin's aim was a separate treaty with Egypt and that the proposal of full autonomy was a cosmetic exercise disguising his intention of holding on to the West Bank and Gaza. For one thing, the autonomy proposal applied only to people and not to land. This prompted Labor Party leader Yigal Allon to remark that only in Marc Chagall's paintings do people float in midair, free from the laws of gravity.

Sadat and Begin had different priorities at Camp David. "Sadat was not particularly interested in the detailed language of the framework for peace," President Carter recalled, "and, with the exception of the settlements, Begin was not very interested in the details of the Sinai agreement."

Egypt's foreign minister, Ibrahim Kamel, resigned, believing Sadat had surrendered on the essential points regarding the West Bank and Gaza and had isolated Egypt from the rest of the Arab world. Jordanians and Palestinians also felt betrayed by Sadat and found the framework agreement unacceptable. The Palestinians rejected the proposal of autonomy, seeing it as a cover for Israeli annexation of the occupied territories with the tacit consent of Egypt and America. They dismissed the offer as little more than Israeli permission to "collect garbage and exterminate mosquitoes."

As Sadat's critics predicted, Egypt went its separate way. On March 26, 1979, the Treaty of Peace between Egypt and Israel was signed in Washington, ending thirty-one years of war. In return for yielding Sinai, Israel secured America's guarantee that it would meet or subsidize Israeli oil requirements and rebuild airfields displaced from the peninsula. A Memorandum of Understanding was also signed, assuring Israel of American support in the event of violations and a continuing commitment to Israel's military and economic requirements.

Under the framework agreement, Israel made what looked like significant concessions. It specifically recognized the "legitimate rights of the Palestinian people," although it continued to deny that the Palestinian people had any right to national self-determination. It also agreed that the Palestinian problem would be resolved "in all its aspects." But Carter gradually drifted into a policy of securing an Egyptian-Israeli treaty at the expense of progress toward his declared goal of a Palestinian homeland. Despite his criticism of Kissinger's step-by-step approach, Carter essentially extended Sinai II to its logical conclusion: the removal of Israeli settlements and the return of the Sinai to Egypt.

The American public hailed the Camp David accords as a triumph for Carter's diplomacy, a departure from America's traditional policy that led to a breakthrough on the Arab-Israeli front. That the package left Israel free to accelerate its creeping annexation of the rest of the occupied territories or to invade Lebanon was not immediately obvious. What at first looked like a diplomatic triumph proved short-lived and shortsighted.

Carter saw the Camp David accords as the first step in a process that would lead to a comprehensive peace between Israel and all its neighbors. But to Menachem Begin, whom Carter once described as a "psycho," the peace with Egypt was not the first step but the end of the road. Begin was con-

In 1994 Israel began to withdraw from the Gaza Strip and Jericho. The borders between Israel and the Palestinian entity and Israel and Syria are subject to negotiations.

vinced that in return for relinquishing Sinai he had secured Israel's right to retain the West Bank and Gaza. Carter was equally convinced that Israel had to return to the 1967 borders on all fronts because the neighboring Arab states were ready for peace, the Palestinians were entitled to a homeland, and "Greater Israel"—that is, an expansionist Israel— would generate perpetual instability in the Middle East. In short, Israel could have territory or peace but not both. In the eyes of many Arabs, Carter's inability to persuade Begin to recognize the legitimate rights of the Palestinian people further discredited the Camp David accords, increased

Egypt's isolation from the rest of the Arab world, and undermined America's credibility as an honest broker between Arabs and Israelis.

When Ronald Reagan entered the White House in 1980, he immediately downplayed the Palestinian problem, emphasized the East-West superpower axis of all international conflicts, and embarked on a new Middle East policy based on four assumptions: first, that the threat to the Persian Gulf's oil-producing countries constituted the central problem facing America; second, that the Arab-Israeli conflict had become less acute and less significant and could therefore remain on the back burner; third, that the Arab-Israeli and Persian Gulf conflicts were distinct, each with its own dynamics and rules, thus making it safe to neglect one and concentrate on the other; and fourth, that the Middle East needed, above all, defense from the Soviet threat. The assumptions were interesting, internally coherent, and completely out of touch with the region's political realities. Nevertheless, the conclusion was that America must organize all its allies, whether Arab or Israeli, in a defensive framework designed to check Soviet advances, to protect the oil producers of the Gulf, and to ensure Western access to the oil. This was the policy of "strategic consensus" much touted in the early days of the Reagan administration, especially by Secretary of State Alexander Haig.

Events, particularly Israel's June 1982 invasion of Lebanon, soon forced the administration to recognize that all the conflicts in the Middle East are important, that they are linked, and that the complex pattern of international politics in the region cannot be reduced to a simple East-West equation.

The Reagan administration supported the invasion and had only itself and Israel to blame for the sequence of reverses and disasters suffered in the invasion's wake. To obtain American support for his plan to create "a new political order" in Lebanon, Israeli defense minister Ariel Sharon emphasized that the new order would weaken the pro-Soviet forces in the Middle East: Syria and the PLO. Alexander Haig's strong anti-Soviet views, his tendency to look upon Middle East issues from a globalist perspective, and his conception of Israel as a strong and dependable strategic ally all facilitated Sharon's task. At their meeting in mid-May 1982, Haig indicated that the United States would not oppose a limited Israeli military operation in Lebanon, provided it could be justified. Sharon concluded that he had received a green light and launched the attack in an effort to destroy the PLO and the Syrian-supported forces in Lebanon.

America's high-risk approach to the Lebanese crisis stood in marked contrast to Soviet caution. Whereas America had presented Israel with a blank check, the Soviet Union limited its commitment to defending Syria, refusing to intervene on the side of Syrian forces in Lebanon. Whereas America deployed troops in Beirut (termed a "peacekeeping force") and a naval armada offshore, the Soviets shunned direct military involvement. America seriously underestimated the risks of military intervention in Lebanon and the violent opposition it was bound to provoke from different groups, each of which had its own armed militia. Two radical groups, the Shiites and the Druze, treated the so-called peacekeeping force like any other local militia and blew up the U.S. headquarters in Beirut, killing 241 Marines. It was a heavy and unnecessary price to pay for ignoring the indigenous political, religious, and ethnic sources of tension and for seeing a Soviet shadow behind every Lebanese tree. Moreover, once Reagan understood the price of intervention in support of the Maronites, a Christian sect with secret links to Israel, the administration cut its losses and withdrew its forces from Lebanon. Reagan's decision dealt a terrible blow to America's prestige in the Arab world and left the Soviets with an opportunity for even greater regional influence.

The war in Lebanon proved that the United States could not safely leave the Arab-Israeli dispute on the back burner. A belated product of this realization was Reagan's September 1982 peace plan, calling for the withdrawal of all foreign troops from Lebanon and the establishment of self-government by the West Bank Palestinians in association with Jordan. But Begin's government predictably and emphatically rejected the Reagan plan. Israel's main purpose in invading Lebanon was to destroy the PLO, thus weakening Palestinian nationalism enough to absorb the West Bank into Greater Israel. After Reagan proposed his plan, Israel used the continuing crisis in Lebanon to block American-sponsored negotiations on the future of the West Bank.

To settle the Lebanese conflict, Haig's successor,

George Shultz, negotiated the May 1983 accord, which gave Israel the right to remain in Lebanon until the Syrians withdrew but ignored completely Syria's interests in Lebanon. When Syria denounced the accord and sponsored attempts to topple Lebanon's Maronite president, Amin Gemayel, Shultz concluded that Syria was the area's chief troublemaker. The Reagan administration, however, was split so many ways that it began to resemble the factionalism of the Middle East itself. Secretary of State Shultz advocated the use of force to make Syria agree to the accord, while Secretary of Defense Caspar Weinberger expounded the virtues of diplomacy. Shultz argued that Syria would agree only if it was clear that America and Israel stood together. In other words, he saw Israel as a strategic asset. The rival school of thought, led by Weinberger, considered Israel a liability. According to Weinberger, the goodwill of the Arab moderates was essential to protect America's Gulf interests, in particular its access to oil, and close military and economic links with Israel would jeopardize this goodwill.

Cold Warrior Ronald Reagan ruled in favor of the first school of thought. A national security directive signed by Reagan in October 1983 reflected Shultz's conviction that the United States had to reaffirm its relationship with Israel to enhance its security interests in the Middle East.

The close cooperation between America and Israel and the joint policy of toughness vis-à-vis Syria yielded effects opposite to those expected. The American view that there was a Soviet-Syrian-

PLO-Druze-Shiite front that could be checked only by means of an American-Israeli-Maronite front was simplistic, particularly given the diversity of interests at play inside each coalition. By insisting on the May 17 accord, the Reagan administration inadvertently helped isolate and weaken President Gemayel and strengthen his Druze and Shiite opponents. By taking military actions against these radical forces, the administration made them more dependent on Syria and helped Syrian president Hafez al-Assad emerge as the real arbiter of Lebanese politics. And by treating the Lebanese civil war and Syria's role in it as a local manifestation of the East-West conflict, the administration forced President Assad and his allies ever more deeply into Moscow's arms.

Reagan's eagerness to place the whole saga behind him is understandable. But the lessons concerning America's role in the Middle East are too striking to be obscured and too important to be forgotten. In the first place, the Lebanon war showed Israel to be not a bastion of stability but a source of regional turmoil and violence, not a strategic asset but a serious liability. Second, despite its concern for regional stability, America contributed to the destruction of the Lebanese state and to the collapse of the already precarious regional order. The third and most significant lesson of the war is that America's uncritical support of Israeli security, as defined by the Israeli government, seriously damaged America's broader interests, those of limiting the influence of the Soviet Union and its radical allies and of expanding its rapport with the moderate

Arab states. America could afford to make mistakes in Lebanon; a superpower enjoys a larger margin of error than a small power. But the fact that the Reagan administration managed to extricate itself from the Lebanese quagmire does not detract from the folly of its involvement. More than any other episode, the Lebanon war exposed the bankruptcy of globalism and the Israel-first approach as a framework for formulating American policy toward the Middle East.

C H A P T E R 4

REALPOLITIK
IN THE GULF

The Cold War outlook that dictated America's policy toward the Arab-Israeli conflict from the Eisenhower administration on also guided its approach to the Persian Gulf. A Gulf policy was simpler to formulate, however, because Israel's security was not directly involved. In the Gulf, America had only two major interests: to bolster the independence, security, and stability of the oil-producing states, thus ensuring access to their vast oil resources, and to contain the spread of Soviet military power and influence. These mutually reinforcing objectives pointed to the preservation of the political status quo. The problem of reconciling America's commitment to Israel with other U.S. interests did not arise in the Gulf. Hence the persistent American attempt to treat the Arab-Israeli problems and those of the Persian Gulf as separate and unrelated.

Superficially, American policy, particularly policy on Soviet containment, may look like an extension of Britain's approach throughout the nineteenth century, but the stakes were different. Britain's involvement in the Gulf started for strategic reasons and gradually encompassed politics and economics; America's involvement started for economic reasons and later encompassed politics and security. Britain paid close attention to local and regional threats to the status quo, whereas America focused on the Soviet threat. The British conception of Gulf security was intimately linked to regional politics and the internal conditions of individual states; the American conception was more closely linked to military alliances, balance of power, and arms supplies.

Before Britain's withdrawal from east of Suez, President Nixon exaggerated the power vacuum such a move would create. By doing so, he hoped to overcome congressional opposition to funding the Indian Ocean military facility closest to the Saudi oil fields. The more critical area, however, was in and around Iran, the center of much of the world's oil production. Britain was no longer willing to defend the area, and America, mired in the costly and unpopular Vietnam War, was unable. But Mohammad Reza Pahlavi, shah of Iran since 1941, was eager to become the Gulf's policeman, a role President Nixon and Henry Kissinger encouraged him to play.

America's disillusion with its part in the Vietnam War led to the 1969 Nixon Doctrine: America would overcome the political and economic

constraints on its power by relying on friendly local powers as regional policemen. In the Middle
East, two candidates nominated themselves for
this role: Israel and Iran. Iran became the key pillar of support for American interests in the Gulf, a
bastion of regional stability and a protector of the
status quo. The United States selected Saudi Arabia as the other pillar in what became known as
the "two-pillar" strategy.

The two-pillar policy implied equal reliance on
Iran and Saudi Arabia, the largest and wealthiest
pro-Western monarchies. But given Saudi Arabia's
limited military capability, the United States acknowledged that Iran would have to be the main
source of strength. Another difficulty was the
quarrelsome relationship between the two pillars.
The Saudi royal family was jealous of the Iranian
dynasty and expressed it in petty and petulant
ways, like calling the Persian Gulf the Arabian
Gulf. Moreover, Saudi Arabia was not just a Gulf
power; it was also a member of the Arab League
and an enemy of Israel. Iran, Islamic but not Arab,
enjoyed covert cooperation with Israel. Iran supplied Israel with oil, while Israel supplied Iran with
arms and related services. Iran did not participate
in the 1973 oil boycott of countries supporting Israel. Israel in turn supported Iran in the Iran-Iraq
War, which lasted from 1980 to 1988. Regarding
oil, however, Americans were closer to the moderate Saudis than to the shah, who pressed for higher
prices and a higher share of the revenues. The two-
pillar policy was thus more problematic than its

name suggests. It was subjected to two severe tests, in 1973–74 and in 1978–79.

Under the two-pillar strategy, America extended a security commitment as well as arms and technical assistance to both Iran and Saudi Arabia. The quality and quantity of arms supplied to the shah, whose policy was to buy the best equipment in the largest possible quantities, increased at a staggering pace. American policy was to indulge rather than curb the shah's desire for arms. Fear of Soviet advances, particularly in Iraq, outweighed restraint. During a May 1972 visit to Tehran, Nixon and Kissinger agreed to let the shah purchase anything he wanted short of nuclear weapons. By the mid-1970s Iran accounted for half of American arms sales abroad, and arms sales became the central component in U.S.-Iranian relations. The sales increased as American companies scrambled for lucrative contracts, contributing to Iranian domestic problems. The overspending on arms led to inflation and corruption as some American company officials offered "commissions" in return for government contracts. The increased exposure to Western ideas also disturbed Islamic fundamentalists. All these factors progressively alienated the Iranian people from their ruler.

Nixon and Kissinger tolerated the shah's repression of human rights such as freedom of speech because he was the only card they had to play against the Soviet Union in Central Asia. They used him to weaken the Soviet Union and its allies, especially Iraq, where secular Arab militants—the Ba'athists—had gained power in 1968. The United States pointed to Soviet arms supplies to Iraq to justify its own policy toward Iran. Although the Soviets made various arms-control proposals, Nixon and Kissinger refused to give them any say in Gulf affairs. They, not the Soviets, were therefore primarily responsible for the unbridled superpower rivalry and for the dangerous escalation of the arms race that accompanied it.

Nixon and Kissinger also aided the shah in his campaign to destabilize the Ba'ath regime in Baghdad. In 1972 they agreed to covert American-Israeli-Iranian action in support of the Kurdish rebels in northern Iraq. A report four years later by the House Select Committee on Intelligence Activities revealed the calculations behind this policy:

> Documents in the committee's possession clearly show that the president, Dr. Kissinger, and the foreign head of state [the shah] hoped that our clients [the Kurds] would not prevail. They preferred instead that the insurgents simply continue a level of hostilities sufficient to sap the resources of our ally's neighboring country [Iraq]. This policy was not imparted to our clients, who were encouraged to continue fighting.

The White House policy treated the Kurds as pawns in a geopolitical game, supporting them only as long as they were useful. America tilted now toward Iran; it would tilt in favor of Iraq when circumstances changed and when it deemed such a tilt advantageous. In the long run this strategy built suspicion and resentment of America on all sides. But its architects were oblivious to the long-term consequences.

In 1973, just as the United States deemed the Nixon Doctrine a success, the Yom Kippur War broke out between Israel and Egypt allied with Syria. The Arab Gulf states made a dramatic and unexpectedly effective contribution to the Egyptian-Syrian war effort by restricting the production and export of oil to America and other supporters of Israel. The action caused panic and disarray in the Western camp; the American policy of separating the Arab-Israeli conflict from relations with the Gulf states lay in ruins, as did the separation of business from politics. By the end of 1974, the Organization of Petroleum Exporting Countries (OPEC), supported by Iran and Saudi Arabia, had raised the price of oil fourfold. The balance of power between the Arabs and the West was about to tilt in favor of the Arabs.

One consequence of the 1973–74 oil shock was a massive transfer of resources from the industrialized countries to the oil producers. The Arab states used their mounting revenues to buy arms, goods, and services from the West and to invest in its financial markets. This created a new kind of linkage between the Western and Gulf economies. Western governments became eager to boost their exports. Consumer demand, led by the shah, and the push of Western arms manufacturers propelled arms transfers in particular. Iran and Saudi Arabia alone ordered $30 billion of American arms between 1973 and 1980. The Gulf became heavily militarized without any perceptible gain in either regional security or internal stability. America committed a serious error in flooding the Gulf with the most advanced weapons, and the local rulers committed an even more serious one by squandering their wealth on military hardware.

Countless disputes over land, water, and oil persisted among the Gulf states following the British withdrawal. The most persistent and dangerous of these pitted Iran against Iraq for control of the strategically vital Shatt al-Arab waterway, which lies along the borders between the two countries. Britain had done well by Iraq in persuading Iran to sign a 1937 agreement that set the border on Shatt al-Arab's eastern shore. In 1969, after Saddam Hussein's Ba'ath Party assumed power, Iran renounced the 1937 treaty and began to challenge Iraqi control of Shatt al-Arab. In 1975 Saddam, the Iraqi vice president and strongman of the regime, concluded an agreement with the shah of Iran that set the border along the median line of the waterway. In return the shah and his American backers agreed to end their support of the Kurdish insurgency in northern Iraq, thus exposing the Kurds to the tender mercies of the Ba'ath regime. It was not the first time America betrayed the Kurds, nor was it to be the last.

Nixon defined security in military terms. Jimmy Carter's presidency emphasized morality. Two important Carter policies resulting from that emphasis—human rights and restrictions on arms sales—threatened the cozy relationship with the shah. Yet U.S.-Iranian relations maintained a remarkable continuity despite the transition from Republican to Democratic rule. One reason for this was the permanent bureaucracy that sustained American defense commitments and regional strategy. Another was that Jimmy Carter appreciated Iran's importance to Western oil supplies, both as a major exporter and as a regional power. There was no obvious alternative to close relations with the shah. What Carter did bring about was a subtle shift in the two-pillar policy, relying more heavily on Saudi Arabia than on Iran.

Carter and his aides thought that a new regional stability had begun. But they misunderstood the process of internal change that led to the 1979 overthrow of the Pahlavi dynasty. No sooner had Carter pronounced Iran an "island of stability" than a revolution forced the shah out of the country. Carter and his advisers were surprised to discover that a large army, police force, and security apparatus could not save the Peacock Throne. They failed to grasp until too late that although the shah had built up his armed forces to assert Iran's independence, most Iranians believed his policy served only his regime and perpetuated their country's dependence on America. Confusion in Washington and conflicting signals during this critical period may also have emboldened the opposition forces and contributed to the shah's downfall.

Carter's ambivalent policy toward the shah explains why both globalists and regionalists have blamed him for the "loss" of Iran. Globalists on the right blamed his human-rights policy and his failure to stand by the shah against Iran's domestic opponents. Regionalists dismissed Carter's human-rights policy as more bark than bite. They blamed him for not persuading the shah to liberalize his regime and for pandering to the shah's whims with unlimited arms supplies. Both globalists and regionalists exaggerate America's influence. The shah's fall was due more to his own domestic and foreign policies than to American policy. As Iran expert R. K. Ramazani has argued, it was not America that lost Iran but the shah who "wooed, won, but also lost America."

With the collapse of the shah's regime, a decade of efforts to develop a viable Gulf strategy ended in spectacular failure. The main prop of the Nixon Doctrine in the region had been demolished. America lost not only prestige, credibility, and a close ally but also its links with the Iranian military, its monitoring stations near the Soviet frontier, and one of its most lucrative export markets. Even more serious, the oil-price increase from $13 to $34 a barrel had profound consequences for the world economy.

At first Carter made an effort to come to terms with the new regime of the elderly and inflexible Ayatollah Ruholla Khomeini. Khomeini had been an outspoken critic of the shah's subservience to America and of his alliance with Israel, regarding both as inimical to Islam. He promptly severed contacts with Israel, and when Iranian students took American diplomats hostage at the Tehran embassy, he severed relations with America as well. An abortive U.S. military mission to free the hostages further embittered relations and dealt another blow to American prestige.

The Islamic revolution reversed Iran's traditional foreign policy, turning America and other former allies into enemies. Iran's new leaders were ideologically opposed to the status quo both at home and in the international system. They believed their revolution would not be secure until Saudi Arabia and Iran's other neighbors threw off American protection. A fundamental tenet of the revolution was that Iran had a God-given mission to export the Islamic system of government to the corrupt pro-Western and anti-Islamic countries of the Persian Gulf. While denouncing America as "the Great Satan," however, the new leaders did not embrace the Soviet Union. On the contrary, they regarded the superpowers as equally guilty of imperialism and sought to free the region from the stranglehold of both. Ayatollah Khomeini's "neither East nor West" was not a mere slogan but a central principle in revolutionary Iran's foreign policy. It implied the creation of an Islamic bloc powerful enough to stand up to both superpowers. This is why the Soviet Union did not welcome the revolution. But to the Americans the new regime was threatening because it challenged the status quo and legitimacy of America's conservative allies in the Gulf.

The Soviet invasion of Afghanistan in December 1979 heightened American unease. For the first time since World War II, large numbers of Soviet troops were committed outside the communist bloc. The effect was to eliminate a buffer state and bring the Red Army closer to the Indian Ocean and the oil fields of the Persian Gulf. Washington feared that the invasion was a prelude to Soviet expansion in the Gulf.

President Carter articulated this concern in his January 1980 State of the Union address: "Let our position be absolutely clear. An attempt by any outside force to gain control of the Persian Gulf will be regarded as an assault on the vital interests of the United States of America, and such an assault will be repelled by any means necessary, including military force." This declaration, which quickly became known as the Carter Doctrine, clarified what American presidents had been saying since 1947. It also bore a striking resemblance to the Lansdowne Declaration of 1903, in which the British foreign secretary of the day warned rival great powers to keep out of the Persian Gulf.

Influenced by events in the "Arc of Crisis," which stretched from Afghanistan to Iran, South Yemen, and Ethiopia, President Carter's foreign policy shifted from regionalism to globalism. Having begun his presidency emphasizing the need to resolve regional disputes and cooperate with the Soviet Union, Carter ended it by focusing on the threat of Soviet expansionism. At the time Carter issued his portentous statement, the American capacity for projecting military power into the Gulf was limited; there had been no military draft for several years, and the United States had no bases in the Gulf. Although Carter emphasized the build-up of the Rapid Deployment Force, a well-trained force able to go anywhere on short notice, it had hardly progressed by the end of his presidency.

On September 22, 1980, shortly before Carter left office, Iraq launched a massive attack on Iran. The animosity between America and the Khomeini regime gave rise to a conspiracy theory that implicated the Carter administration as an accomplice. Iranians of all factions believed that Great Satan encouraged the attack. Some liberal critics of America also believed this theory. Christopher Hitchens, Washington editor of *Harper's Magazine*, for example, charged that America knew Iraq was planning an assault on a neighboring country and, at the very least, took no steps to prevent it.

Upon close inspection, however, the circumstantial evidence pointing to an independent Iraqi decision outweighs the conjectural. Saddam Hussein, by now president of Iraq, had the motives, the military capability, and the opportunity to attack Iran. The motives were to settle old scores with an ancient foe, assert control over the disputed Shatt al-Arab waterway, and establish primacy in the Gulf. The provocative behavior of the new Iranian regime, especially its call to Iraqi Shiites to overthrow Saddam and establish an Islamic state like Iran's, supplied another Iraqi motive for war. The rupture between revolutionary Iran and its principal source of arms and spare parts enhanced Iraq's military advantage. And the chaotic state of affairs within Iran after the revolution led Saddam Hussein to believe, erroneously as it turned out,

71

that he could achieve swift victory. Saddam thus needed no encouragement from America or anyone else to launch his war on Iran.

America's Persian Gulf policy oscillated during the 1970s from the globalism of the Nixon administration to the regionalism of the early days of the Carter administration and back toward globalism at the end of Carter's term. Numerous events challenged America's position during this decade: the Yom Kippur War, the oil shocks, the full-scale Iranian revolution, and the 1980 Iran-Iraq War. All these threats to oil supplies and regional stability sprang from within. None could be blamed on the Soviet Union. There was thus some inconsistency in Carter's adoption of the Soviet-instigation argument as the basis of American planning for defense of the Gulf. It was left to his Republican successor, however, to use this argument as the basis for America's entire global strategy in what came to be known as the Second Cold War.

TILTING
TOWARD IRAQ

One of the paradoxes of the tragic encounter between America and Iran is that Ronald Reagan may have owed his 1980 election to the fiercely anti-American clerics in Tehran. Just as Jimmy Carter, according to one conspiracy theory, was an accomplice in the Iraqi attack on Iran, the Reagan campaign, according to a second conspiracy theory, made a deal with Iran to release the American hostages. The difference is that the first conspiracy theory is not credible, and the second is. In his book *October Surprise,* Gary Sick, a member of the National Security Council under Presidents Ford, Carter, and Reagan, argues that members of the Reagan campaign negotiated a secret deal delaying the release of the hostages until after the election. In return, and in the event of a Republican victory, Israel would sell arms and spare parts to Iran with

American acquiescence. Iran, locked in war with Iraq, was in desperate need of arms. Israel wanted to prolong the war as a way of keeping its adversaries occupied. And America was obsessed with the hostage crisis.

The fate of the hostages was a central issue in the 1980 election. They had been seized in November 1979 by followers of Ayatollah Khomeini. An April 1980 military effort to release them failed. Reagan campaign officials worried that Carter would obtain the hostages' release through negotiations or a second rescue mission before election day. Vice-presidential candidate George Bush called the possibility of a second mission Carter's October Surprise. In fact, Iran announced the hostages' release exactly five minutes after Ronald Reagan took the oath of office. The exposure of a similar arms-for-hostages swap five years later—the Iran-Contra affair—deepened public suspicion that the Reagan-Bush campaign had struck its first deal with Iran in October 1980.

Several years of research, including hundreds of interviews in the United States, Europe, and the Middle East, enabled Sick to piece together portions of the tangled story. According to his theory, in July 1980 William J. Casey, Reagan's campaign manager and later director of the Central Intelligence Agency, met with Mehdi Karrubi, Khomeini's representative, in a Madrid hotel. There the pair allegedly began discussion of an arms deal that was completed when the two sides met again in Paris the following October.

A ten-month investigation by the House Foreign Affairs Committee, however, concluded in January 1993 that there was no credible evidence of unauthorized communications between the Reagan campaign and Iran or any plan to delay the hostages' release. Still, a Senate report that followed acknowledged that unanswered questions about Casey's activities remained. Because his activities are central to Sick's accusations, some government officials and political analysts continue to believe the allegations.

The October Surprise, if true, would be a terrible indictment of Reagan and his associates. It would suggest that they were not above tampering with foreign policy for partisan advantage and, in doing so, running the risk of blackmail by Iran and Israel. Most disturbing, it would suggest that the Iran-Contra affair was implicit in the Reagan-Bush approach to foreign policy.

Several months after taking office, the Reagan administration reversed Carter's embargo on arms to Iran by allowing Israel to sell several billion dollars' worth of American-made arms, spare parts, and ammunition to Iran. Although a *New York Times* inquiry found no link between these arms sales and the October Surprise allegation, it did note that the U.S. government authorized Israel to make the sales on a case-by-case basis and that the arrangement was terminated in the spring of 1982 when Israel began selling American-made equipment without Washington's permission. But arms sales to Iran via Israel continued unchecked despite

the revoked agreement and Operation Staunch, a
mid-eighties initiative by the Reagan administration to curb arms transfers to Iran.

That Israel had such influence on America's Persian Gulf policy is surprising given the administration's insistence that relations with the Gulf states
were a separate issue from the Arab-Israeli conflict. The Cold War outlook, however, drove the
foreign policy of the Reagan administration.
Ronald Reagan spent many sleepless afternoons in
the White House worrying about the Soviet threat.
In the Middle East and the Gulf, his foreign policy
aimed to exclude Soviet influence, and Israel was
seen as a strategic asset in pursuit of this goal.

Yet the Reagan administration's policy toward
the Gulf and in particular toward Iran was erratic
and contradictory, the result of competing and often conflicting objectives pursued by three groups
of officials: those prepared to combat the Soviet
Union, those who emphasized the special relationship with Israel, and those primarily concerned
with access to oil and economic opportunities in
the Arab states. Reagan's idleness, intellectual
mediocrity, and lax leadership gave these groups
unusual latitude, which sometimes resulted in the
left hand's ignorance of what the right hand was
doing.

Reagan's presidency roughly coincided with the
Iran-Iraq War, which became the center stage of
America's Gulf policy. Initially Reagan continued
Carter's posture of neutrality and the ban on the
sale of military equipment to either. But during the
course of his presidency, he and his advisers broke

this ban by supplying arms to both nations, some-times simultaneously. In the early days, however, America was equally hostile to Iran and Iraq. Indeed, Americans would have been hard put to say which side they wanted to see defeated. Henry Kissinger summed up the general preference when he indicated that the best outcome would be for both sides to lose.

America viewed Iraq as an agent of Soviet subversion and Iran as radical and therefore a potential Soviet proxy as well, despite its "neither East nor West" policy. Imprisoned in its self-made ideological straitjacket, the Reagan administration misinterpreted the Soviet role in the Iran-Iraq War and overlooked the opportunities for superpower collaboration to promote their common interests. Neither welcomed the Iranian revolution, neither trusted the Khomeini regime, and neither wanted an Iranian victory in the Iran-Iraq War. They also shared responsibility for preventing the war's escalation.

The Soviet Union condemned Iraq for starting the war, suspended arms supplies, and agreed to remain neutral. It saw the war as something harmful to both sides and wanted to bring it to an end. Only in 1982, when Iran invaded Iraqi territory, did Moscow resume arms supplies to Iraq, simultaneously urging a peaceful settlement.

The Reagan administration, however, was reluctant to develop cooperative Gulf policies within the competitive relationship with the Soviets. The Cold Warriors, in short, became Gulf Warriors and blocked the avenue of superpower collaboration. The Gulf was in effect a strategic chessboard on which the superpowers played out their conflict, ignoring the local sources of conflict. Reagan and his advisers reduced American policy to one imperative: the containment of a putative Soviet military threat.

As Reagan's globalism dominated the policy-making agenda, the Gulf rose among his administration's priorities. A Pentagon statement of defense priorities for 1984–88 ranked the defense of the Middle and Near East as second only to that of North America and Western Europe:

> Our principle [sic] objectives are to assure continued access to Persian Gulf oil and to prevent the Soviets from acquiring political-military control of the oil directly or through proxies. It is essential that the Soviet Union be confronted with the prospect of a major conflict should it seek to reach oil resources of the Gulf. Whatever the circumstances, we should be prepared to introduce American forces directly into the region should it appear that the security of access to Persian Gulf oil is threatened.

Two events in 1982 brought about a reappraisal of American globalist policy: Israel's invasion of Lebanon and Iran's successful counteroffensive against Iraq. Secretary of State Alexander Haig's policy of "strategic consensus" had been based on a series of assumptions—that the Soviet Union posed the single greatest threat to American interests in the Middle East, that the countries in the region agreed on the need to counter this threat, and that the United States could separate Gulf conflict from Arab-Israeli conflict and keep the latter on the back burner while concentrating on what it considered more important objectives. The two events called all these assumptions into question, and the administration began to see Israel not as a help but as a cause of Arab dependence on the Soviet Union.

Another casualty of the Lebanon war was Alexander Haig, the principal architect of the globalist approach. Following his resignation, Washington shifted toward a regionalist approach, recognizing that America could no longer ignore the Arab-Israeli conflict nor prevent it from impinging on America's relations with the Gulf states. Access to oil continued to rank as America's most vital interest, but America recognized anew its dependence on Arab goodwill and the resulting need to resolve the Arab-Israeli conflict. Hoping that Iraq would eventually join the moderates led by Egypt and Saudi Arabia, America began to cultivate a bloc of moderate Arab states.

The shift in the American attitude toward Iraq had its more immediate roots, however, in events on the Iraqi-Iranian border. The Iranian counter-offensive launched in March 1982 expanded both the war and Iranian war aims, which now included overthrowing Saddam Hussein. In Washington the fear of an Iranian victory and a consequent spread of Islamic fundamentalism overtook the fear of an Iraqi victory that might further Soviet advances.

The struggle for mastery between Iran and Iraq also assumed an ideological aspect, pitting Iran, the leader of revolutionary Islam, against secular Iraq, the defender of the status quo and the champion of Arab unity.

Fear of an Iranian military victory, reinforced by the fear of ideological victory for revolutionary and expansionist Islam, led America to abandon its neutrality of the previous two years and start tilting toward Iraq. The aim of American intervention, wrote Reagan national security adviser Robert C. McFarlane in the *Los Angeles Times,* was "to prevent either side from winning and . . . to bring them both to a negotiated settlement in which we could reestablish over time a stable relationship with Iran—the strategic prize of the area."

American-Iraqi relations developed in three stages. From 1982 to 1984 America provided political support and allowed Iraq to purchase American commodities on credit. Between 1984 and 1986 the United States resumed arms sales to Iraq and restored diplomatic relations after a seventeen-year hiatus. From 1986 to 1988 the two formed a tacit alliance in which America became Iraq's defender of last resort in the Gulf.

An effort to contain Iran militarily accompanied the diplomatic tilt toward Iraq. The administration launched Operation Staunch to slow down arms shipments to Iran and encouraged France to keep Iraq supplied with fighter planes and missiles. The Gulf states, with American encouragement, allowed Iraq to continue its expensive arms purchases on credit. And America led the condemnation of Iran at the UN and other international forums but remained silent when Iraq started to attack ships using Iranian ports. Indeed, America took advantage of the "tanker war" to send more warships into the Gulf and to upgrade Saudi Arabia's air defense. The message to Tehran was that America would not stand idly by while Iran tried to intimidate America's Gulf allies.

Closer military and intelligence cooperation marked the second stage, which opened with the December 1984 restoration of diplomatic relations. Iraq seized the military initiative, and the pendulum of the Iran-Iraq War began to swing in Iraq's favor. America had two alternatives for inducing Iran to negotiate the war's end. It could either intensify the military pressure on Iran by stepping up its support for Iraq, or it could provide incentives for negotiation. By 1985 two groups of officials were pursuing these alternative policies simultaneously, with disastrous results. One group, which included Secretary of Defense Caspar Weinberger, saw Iran as the main threat to America's Gulf interests and advocated a policy of cooperation with Iraq and other friendly Arab regimes to contain this threat. The other group, which included national security advisers Richard V. Allen, Robert McFarlane, and Admiral John M. Poindexter, believed Iran was basically more hostile to the USSR than to America. By covertly supplying arms to Iran, they sought to encourage Iranian moderates and to secure the release of

Americans taken hostage by Iran's allies in Lebanon. While maintaining the official policy of confronting Iran diplomatically and militarily, this second group initiated a covert policy of selling arms to Iran with the help of Israel.

Americans, including the architects of Middle East policy, were shocked by the November 1986 revelation of the arms sales to Iran. America's credibility in the eyes of its Arab allies was seriously damaged. At home the revelations ignited a political crisis that acquired the label "Irangate" because of the similarity it bore to the Watergate scandal that had destroyed the presidency of Richard Nixon. Irangate was also known as the Iran-Contra affair, because despite the express prohibition of Congress, officials had diverted the profits from the illicit arms sales to the Contras, a rebel army fighting the left-wing government in Nicaragua. Congressional and public attacks on the Reagan administration forced it to abandon its arms-for-hostages policy and its covert support for the Contras and Iran.

The Iran-Contra scandal revealed the Reagan administration at its worst, not simply unscrupulous in its conduct of foreign policy but also undemocratic and incompetent. By agreeing to swap arms for hostages, the administration defeated its own policy of combating international terrorism. The ayatollahs attributed the Reagan administration's agreement to sell weapons to Iran and to press Kuwait for the release of Islamic terrorists to their own firmness. The lesson they must have drawn was that further military pressure on Iraq and further support for international terrorism would yield further American concessions. If America was either so weak or so fickle as to tilt against Iraq under pressure, why doubt that it could be made to tilt again?

An American swing back toward Iraq characterized the third stage, which lasted from 1986 until the Iran-Iraq cease-fire in 1988. America intervened more actively in the war and became the ultimate guarantor of Iraqi security. Iran's capture of the Fao peninsula in February 1986 was the catalyst that pushed America into a tacit alliance with Iraq. Located at Iraq's southernmost point, the Fao peninsula was a critical area for the Iraqi oil industry. The fall of the peninsula raised the specter of an Iranian thrust to Basra and a possible dismemberment of the Iraqi state that Britain had created out of three Ottoman provinces after World War I. America responded by giving Iraq more intelligence assistance and protecting Kuwaiti tankers from Iranian attacks.

The Reagan administration's decision to provide a naval escort to Kuwaiti oil tankers involved America in an open-ended military commitment despite considerable congressional opposition. Some commentators have agreed that as Iraq's ally, Kuwait manipulated America with the aim of getting America into the middle of the Iran-Iraq War. Others take the view that the military commitment resulted from the decision to support Iraq in its war against Iran. The Kuwaiti request simply gave America a convenient excuse to expand its presence and to protect Iraq and its allies. An element of truth lies in both views: Kuwait was certainly manipulative, and the Reagan administration was predisposed to increasing its military presence in the Gulf despite the risks. An inflated U.S. assessment of Soviet aims and influence goes a long way in explaining this controversial decision.

The sequence of events was as follows: In December 1986 Kuwait asked both superpowers to protect its oil tankers by placing them under their flags. The assumption was that a superpower flag would deter the Iranians from attacking. The Soviet Union was willing to lease three oil tankers flying the Soviet flag to Kuwait. In March, however, the Reagan administration said it would either take on the whole job of reflagging or do nothing at all. It would not go "halvies" with the Russians. The result: America reflagged eleven Kuwaiti tankers, qualifying them for American naval escorts. Several European countries, including Britain and France, provided tanker escorts as well. The U.S. all-or-nothing response was clearly intended to restrict the Soviet naval presence in the Gulf.

The lesson, which Kuwait and the other vulnerable Arab Gulf states were not slow to learn, was that the easiest way to manipulate the Reagan administration was to turn to Moscow. Ironically, of the six conservative states that banded together in 1981 to form the Gulf Cooperation Council—founded in self-defense following the Soviet invasion of Afghanistan and in fear of Iranian victory in its war with Iraq—Kuwait had been the most outspoken critic of American presence in the Gulf and the foremost advocate of accommodation with the Soviet Union.

The reflagging operation contributed little to the safety of Gulf commerce. The more significant effect was to pave the way for an expanded American naval presence. A few months later the Reagan administration sent American vessels to patrol the Gulf and to escort tanker convoys to and from Kuwait. The United States Navy did not protect the ships of other countries against Iranian attacks, nor did it stop Iraq from using sophisticated Western weapons against civilian craft. America was interested in freedom of navigation only for Kuwait, Iraq, and its other allies, and in limiting Soviet involvement. But doing the job the American way increased the risk of a military confrontation involving the American navy.

On May 17, 1987, an Iraqi missile accidentally hit the U.S. frigate *Stark*. President Reagan reacted by issuing a warning to the Soviet Union and virtually declaring war on Iran. In a May 29 speech, he spoke of the Soviet Union and Iran as if they were guilty of a plot to sabotage the freedom of navigation in the Gulf. They had to be prevented from "imposing their will on the friendly Arab states of the Persian Gulf," he stressed, and Iran had to be deterred from "blocking the free passage of neutral shipping." He never mentioned Iraq. The irony of blaming Iran for a shot fired by Iraq was not lost on some observers. The most charitable explanation, suggested by one British diplomat, was that Reagan could not tell the difference between the two big *I*'s, Iran and Iraq. On the day of Reagan's speech, Richard Murphy, assistant secretary of state for Near Eastern Affairs, told the Senate Foreign Relations Committee that "what is driving our policy at this point [is that] we don't want the Soviets to get a handle on a vital lifeline" of the world's oil supply. It was a remarkably frank admission.

While the Iraqi missile attack on the U.S.S. *Stark* was hardly a logical reason for denying the Soviet Union a role in the Gulf, the incident did underline the pressing need for a solution to the Iran-Iraq conflict. Discussions among Security Council members had been going on since January, and America took the lead. The declared aim of its policy was to secure a negotiated settlement. But its method, far from being evenhanded, was to take sides more unambiguously than before, to throw its weight onto the Iraqi side, to give Iraq economic, diplomatic, and intelligence assistance, and to intervene militarily, attacking such Iranian targets as the Sirri oil platform. America became a belligerent in the Iran-Iraq War in all but name.

By taking sides America hoped to pressure Iran into accepting a cease-fire, but instead the war lasted another six months, in part because Iran was reluctant to submit to American pressure. America's bias against Iran strengthened the position of Iranian hard-liners who wanted to continue the war. And the Security Council's July 1987 resolution calling for an end to the war was unacceptable to Iran, which kept demanding the removal of Saddam from office. As negotiations bogged down, the United States concentrated on establishing an arms embargo against Iran. This gave Iraq the opportunity to launch a series of brutal and devastatingly effective offensives that included the use of chemical weapons against civilian targets. The attacks demoralized Iran and on July 18, 1988, it formally accepted Resolution 598. Two days later Ayatollah Khomeini, in a speech to his nation, justified the decision, which he called "more deadly than taking poison."

The Reagan administration's policy toward Iran and Iraq was neither coherent nor consistent. Its eight years in power make a sorry tale of floundering and blundering, of dishonesty and deception, of expediency and myopia. The worst blot on its record was the clandestine policy of swapping arms for hostages. The secretive, erratic, and unconstitutional manner in which the Reagan administration operated, especially in the Iran-Contra affair, led one U.S. journalist to dub the administration "Reagan's junta." America's policy toward Iran left a bitter legacy of suspicion and hostility. Its policy toward Iraq, although inconsistent, ended up by accepting Saddam Hussein as a junior partner in preserving the status quo in the Gulf, another remarkable irony in light of America's subsequent war with Saddam in early 1991.

Reagan's position on the Iran-Iraq War, dominated and distorted by his obsession with the Soviet threat, fueled rather than reduced regional instability. The Iran-Iraq War was the longest international conflict since World War II, and one of the nastiest and costliest, in both money and human lives. It started as a result of rivalries inside rather than outside the region, but Reagan's intervention prolonged it unnecessarily. In the end both sides felt cheated of victory. The Iraqis felt that, had they been allowed to press their attack, they would have destroyed the Khomeini regime. The Iranians felt that, had it been a fair fight, without American intervention, they would have destroyed Saddam's regime. In this sense the war solved nothing. The threat each regime presented the other did not disappear with the cease-fire. The Iranians were not given the satisfaction of a single UN resolution condemning Iraq for starting the war. The hostility between Iran and Iraq, and Iran and America, was as great, if not greater, at the end of the eight-year war as it had been at the beginning.

DESERT SHIELD AND DESERT STORM

Iraq's 1990 invasion of Kuwait can be seen as the last chapter in the Iran-Iraq War. Both invasions were launched by the same Iraqi dictator as part of the same drive for power, wealth, territorial expansion, and military aggrandizement. The second, however, was considerably more serious in that it was an attempt to snuff out an independent state. The West, and indeed the Middle East, responded to each invasion differently: the United States was tolerant of the first and anything but tolerant of the second. The Middle East nations supported Iraq during the Iran-Iraq War, yet, for the most part, joined the American-led coalition against Iraq in the Gulf war.

During the Iran-Iraq War the oil-rich Gulf states and the Western powers, including America, helped create a monster in the shape of Saddam

Hussein. Nevertheless, they expected this monster to behave reasonably after the war, at least as far as their interests were concerned. But on August 2, 1990, Saddam suddenly turned against his makers by seizing Kuwait.

By the end of the Iran-Iraq War, the Reagan administration's view of Iraq had become so rigid, so impervious to conflicting evidence, and so widely held that *The Economist* labeled it "the conception." According to this view, Iraq had become a bastion of regional stability, a moderate, status quo power bent on economic reconstruction rather than on further military adventures. Saddam Hussein had succeeded the shah of Iran as the policeman and guardian of American interests in the Gulf. As far as the Arab-Israeli conflict was concerned, the conception held that Iraq had broken with its rejectionist past and could therefore help America steer the Arab world toward a settlement. In 1982 Iraq had been taken off the State Department's register of governments sponsoring international terrorism; Saddam was viewed as a reformed character.

This conception of a moderate, pro-Western Iraq dominated American policy until Saddam shattered it in the early hours of August 2. Although George Bush reviewed Middle East policy when he took office, his administration was no less convinced than Reagan's that it could do business with Iraq. In January 1990 Bush issued a directive reaffirming the policy of normal relations with Iraq that included the sale of sensitive technology and credits from the Export-Import Bank. Bush's notion of normal relations and his drive to maintain the status quo allowed him to overlook Saddam's brutality—his systematic violation of human rights and his use of poison gas first against Iranian soldiers, then against Iranian civilians, and eventually against his own Kurdish population. American officials would occasionally protest, but their protests were ignored.

The notion of a moderate Iraq also blinded Washington to contradictory signals from Baghdad. In word and deed, Saddam signaled his ambition to dominate the Gulf. Instead of using Iraq's oil revenues to repay $70 billion in war debts, he increased his military capability, developing weapons of mass destruction. Western companies did brisk business with Saddam, and Western governments did little to discourage them. A British diplomat instrumental in formulating his country's policy toward Iraq summed up the attitude of Western governments shortly before the Iraqi invasion of Kuwait. "In a playground full of bullies, Saddam Hussein was the biggest of all," he said. "But he held the keys to the [candy] shop, so we had to stay on his side."

In the first half of 1990, Saddam accompanied his military buildup with verbal assaults on America and its allies. In January he warned fellow Arabs that the Soviet Union's decline meant increased U.S. power in the Gulf, especially over oil prices. On April 2 he threatened to use chemical weapons against Israel. If America thought it could cover an Israeli strike on Iraq, he said, "by God, we will make the fire eat up half of Israel."

Saddam's other major target was Kuwait. He accused Kuwait of stealing Iraqi oil by extracting more than its share from the Rumaila oil field, which straddled the border between the two countries, and of inflicting massive losses in oil revenue on Iraq by exceeding its OPEC production quota, thereby depressing the price. Saddam followed these well-founded complaints with accusations that Kuwait's oil policy amounted to a declaration of economic war that formed part of an American conspiracy to undermine Iraq.

Saddam demanded that Kuwait compensate Iraq for its losses, write off the debt that had accumulated during the war with Iran, settle the border dispute, and allow Iraq better access to the Persian Gulf by leasing it the islands of Warba and Bubiyan. Kuwait adamantly refused. This unyielding stand exasperated Saddam and surprised others because the rulers of Kuwait, the al-Sabah family, were not noted for political courage. On the contrary, the al-Sabahs usually bought their way out of trouble. Some Arab observers concluded that there must have been an American promise to help Kuwait in the event of trouble or even a secret American-Kuwaiti plot to lure Saddam into a trap. No concrete evidence, however, has ever been produced to support this theory.

The real charge against the Bush administration was not that it suddenly got tough with Saddam but that it remained complacent and conciliatory, not to say obsequious, in the face of mounting threats and provocations. Despite all the signs of danger, American policy continued to cruise along the well-charted path of appeasement. On April 12, 1990, a delegation of five senators headed by Republican minority leader Robert Dole visited Baghdad. Dole assured Saddam that Bush wanted to improve relations. April C. Glaspie, the American ambassador present at the meeting, also confirmed that this was U.S. government policy. Later in the month John Kelly, the U.S. assistant secretary of state for Near East and South Asian Affairs, opposed a congressional initiative to place economic sanctions on Iraq; they would penalize American exporters, explained Kelly, without moderating the actions of Iraq.

The policy of appeasement reached its inglorious climax at the famous meeting between the Iraqi president and the American ambassador on July 25. Glaspie listened politely while Saddam ranted about Kuwait's iniquities and threatened to resort to force. She did her best to mollify the angry tyrant and assured him, "We have no opinion on the Arab-Arab conflicts like your border disagreement with Kuwait." Saddam could be forgiven for inferring from this statement that America would remain neutral if he moved against Kuwait, that the response was likely to be jawboning rather than war.

Even when Iraq moved troops to the Kuwaiti border, the view in both Washington and the Middle East was that it was an attempt to extract money rather than a prelude to force. On July 31, three days before the Iraqi troops charged into Kuwait, Kelly testified on Capitol Hill that America had no treaty and no commitment obliging it to send forces should Kuwait be overrun. Whether a warning of American intervention would have deterred Saddam, there is no way of telling; no warning was issued.

One reason for America's complacency was the lack of concern among Gulf rulers, none of whom foresaw that their erstwhile protector against revolutionary Iran was about to turn predator. The Kuwaitis had every opportunity to ask for assistance from the United States, but they delayed doing so, possibly because they suspected that America would use the Iraqi threat to establish a military presence on their soil. The message from America's other Arab allies, like President Hosni Mubarak of Egypt and King Hussein of Jordan, was that this was an Arab crisis to which an Arab solution would be found. Saddam assured these leaders, as well as King Fahd of Saudi Arabia, with whom he had concluded a defense pact in 1989, that he would not attack Kuwait, and they relayed these assurances to Washington. But the Iraq-Kuwait negotiations arranged by the Arab leaders and held in Jidda, Saudi Arabia, turned out to have been a smoke screen. The invasion began just hours after the plane returning the Iraqi negotiators touched down in Baghdad.

Saddam's motives are not hard to fathom. Since most Iraqis had been brought up to think that Kuwait was part of their country, Saddam could pose as the liberator of usurped Iraqi land. In particular, the capture of Kuwait could give Iraq the access to the Gulf that Great Britain had denied when drawing the border back in 1922. The move could also serve Saddam's ambitions to make Iraq the leader of the Arab world and the predominant oil power. But while Iraq had the world's fourth largest army, with more aircraft and tanks than Britain and France combined, it was in financial straits. By capturing Kuwait's fabulous wealth, Saddam probably hoped to solve his financial problems with one stroke.

The Iraqi invasion of Kuwait, said one U.S. officer, was a cakewalk. Around midnight on August 2, 1990, some 100,000 troops poured across the border toward Kuwait City, meeting little resistance. By dawn the encirclement of the capital was complete and the emir of Kuwait had fled to Saudi Arabia. It is said that the only quick decision sheik Jaber al-Ahmed al-Sabah ever made was to leap into his Mercedes-Benz and head south as Iraqi tanks trundled toward his palace. Saddam Hussein had staged a successful military operation, although it would prove to be a major strategic blunder. On the American side the invasion exposed an intelligence failure and, even more serious, a policy failure. A conception ten years in the making was shattered overnight.

Iraq's annexation of Kuwait presented America with a series of challenges—to its interests in oil, to its interests in Saudi Arabia, and to its prestige in the Gulf. It also challenged the old territorial order that the colonial powers had imposed on the region after the breakup of the Ottoman Empire. Saddam claimed, not without reason, that Kuwait was a creation of British imperialism. But the British imperialists had established all Iraq's borders and not just that with Kuwait. By questioning its legitimacy, Saddam was questioning the legitimacy of all Iraq's borders, including the Shatt al-Arab border with Iran, which Britain had settled in Iraq's favor. Using force to change one border would have been a recipe for never-ending turmoil. Finally, the annexation of Kuwait was the first major challenge to the new, post–Cold War order, which America dominated. Each of these challenges was serious enough; the combination ensured that Iraq's aggression would not go unanswered.

President Bush took charge of formulating America's response to these challenges. After all, foreign policy was said to be his strong suit. On the morning of August 2, Bush told reporters, "We're not discussing intervention." But later that day, in Aspen, Colorado, he met with British prime minister Margaret Thatcher, who took a hard line, referring to Saddam as another Hitler. She invoked the lessons of the 1938 Munich Agreement in which the Allies acquiesced to Hitler's takeover of western Czechoslovakia and urged her colleague to take the firmest possible stand. Bush proposed taking the matter to the United Nations. Thatcher reluctantly agreed but added, "This is no time to go wobbly, George." That afternoon Bush condemned Iraq's "naked aggression." On the way to Aspen, Bush had been unsure how to respond to the crisis; on the way back to Washington, he was quite sure that there must be no appeasement, no negotiation, and no compromise.

Bush took charge. From August 2, 1990, until January 16, 1991, when the president launched the air strike against Iraq, he single-mindedly steered the country toward war, overriding the advice of his military experts, who pushed for a strategy of containment, and of his secretary of state, who favored a diplomatic solution.

Although there was no evidence that Saddam intended to march farther south to capture the Saudi oil fields, he had that capability. A former Texas oilman, Bush feared the possible takeover of Saudi Arabia, which would have increased Saddam's control from 20 percent to 40 percent of the world's known oil reserves, thus placing the world at his mercy. The Saudis, however, were reluctant to have American troops on their soil, so the president and his aides had to do considerable arm-twisting to secure Saudi consent. On August 8, after the Saudis had acquiesced, Bush announced that the Saudi government had requested help, and that he had responded to that request. He added, "The mission of our troops is wholly defensive." A press briefing stated that 50,000 troops would be sent to Saudi Arabia, although the plan was to send 250,000. In line with its defensive mission, the deployment was dubbed Operation Desert Shield.

The United Nations supported the American strategy of isolating and containing Iraq. All permanent members of the Security Council, including the Soviet Union, which had substantial investments in Iraq, followed the American lead. During the crisis the Security Council passed several resolutions: Resolution 660, condemning the Iraqi invasion of Kuwait and calling for an immediate and unconditional withdrawal; Resolution 661, imposing economic sanctions against Iraq; and Resolution 678, authorizing the use of "all necessary means" to secure Iraq's removal from Kuwait. Some observers, including former president Richard Nixon in his 1992 book *Seize the Moment,* have argued that during the Gulf crisis and war America used the UN. The point that tends to get lost in this argument is that the American national interest in restoring the old territorial order and denying Saddam control over Gulf oil happened to coincide with the UN principles of collective security. Saddam's move was a textbook example of the kind of aggression the UN had been set up to deal with.

President Bush displayed no interest in a negotiated settlement of the Kuwait crisis. He gave short shrift, for example, to King Hussein's efforts to mediate. The Jordanian king was later to claim that he had been on the verge of securing an Iraqi withdrawal. But this diplomatic initiative—like the subsequent ones by the PLO, Sudan, Yemen, and Tunisia—was unacceptable to America because it implied some sort of reward to Iraq for having violated the territorial integrity of a UN member. From August 2 until November 29, America held its position that Iraq had to implement unconditionally all UN resolutions. The allied embargo, in the words of Crown Prince Hassan of Jordan, was an embargo on dialogue.

Saddam Hussein's peace initiative of August 12, which linked Iraqi withdrawal from Kuwait to Israeli withdrawal from occupied Arab territories, was rejected by America for the same reason: it would have allowed Saddam to benefit from his aggression. Saddam's proposal of linkage between the Palestinian and Kuwaiti problems was as cynical as it was ingenious. It enabled him to pose as the champion of Palestinian rights, it gained him support among the Arab masses, and it even resurfaced a number of times at the United Nations. For the Americans, however, the timing of linkage was all-important. They insisted that the Palestinian problem should be addressed only after Iraq had unconditionally withdrawn from Kuwait, and they refused to let Saddam have a handle on the Palestinian issue. Under the impact of the invasion, American policy toward Saddam had thus swung from the pole of appeasement to that of refusing even to negotiate.

Although many of his military advisers felt the strategy of containment and economic sanction was working, Bush prepared to bomb Iraq. On October 31 he increased the Desert Shield troops to 400,000. This decision was not announced until November 8, after the congressional elections. A week later Bush assured congressional leaders that the troops' mission was still defensive: "I have not crossed any Rubicon," he said. But the Rubicon *had* been crossed. The increase in American ground forces represented the critical transition from Desert Shield to Desert Storm.

On November 29 the Security Council passed Resolution 678, authorizing the use of force to remove Iraq from Kuwait after a goodwill pause of forty-five days. The media promptly dubbed it "the mother of all resolutions." Bush now felt strong enough to "go the extra mile for peace," as he said, by offering either to send Secretary of State James Baker to Baghdad or to have Iraqi foreign minister Tariq Aziz come to Washington. Baker and Aziz eventually met in Geneva on January 9, 1991, but the meeting accomplished nothing. They talked for six hours—one of the longest dialogues of the deaf in recent diplomatic history. Baker handed Aziz a stern letter, in which Bush told Saddam his choice was between complying with UN resolutions and withdrawing peacefully from Kuwait or being expelled by force. Aziz read the letter but declined to pass it on to his boss.

Bush expected the talks to fail. On December 29 he had told General Colin Powell, the chairman of the Joint Chiefs of Staff, to prepare for an attack on Iraq soon after the January 15 UN deadline. By that deadline military units from thirty countries were deployed in the Gulf, a mark of Bush's success in building an international coalition. The allies expected and fervently hoped that Saddam's defeat would lead to his fall from power, although this was not an explicit war aim. The two declared war aims were the removal of the Iraqi forces from Kuwait and the restoration of the legitimate Kuwaiti government.

Operation Desert Storm was launched on January 16 and lasted forty-two days. The air war lasted thirty-eight days and the ground war one hundred hours. Like the Iraqi invasion of Kuwait, the operation was a cakewalk. Iraqi forces put up virtually no resistance. So great was the disparity in the firepower and competence of the two sides that the encounter could hardly be called a war. The only area in which the Iraqi soldiers distinguished themselves was blowing up Kuwaiti oil fields. They did an extremely thorough job of that.

On February 28, when the coalition forces had overrun Kuwait and southern Iraq, and the Iraqi army was in flight, Bush gave the order for a cease-fire. The mother of all battles threatened by Saddam had ended in a military catastrophe. But while Operation Desert Storm was a triumph of advanced military technology against a Third World army that lacked the will to fight, its political aftermath was more problematic. The basic objectives of the operation were achieved: coalition forces had ejected Iraqi forces from Kuwait and restored the government-in-exile. But Saddam retained his power in Baghdad.

During the war Bush repeatedly stated that he would not allow Saddam's government to survive and openly called on the Iraqi people to revolt against their leader. On March 1, the day after the cease-fire, the Shiites rose up in the south, and a few days later the Kurds did the same in the north. If Bush was serious about toppling Saddam, now was his chance. But when the moment arrived, Bush recoiled from pursuing his policy to its logical conclusion. On March 26, James Baker and National Security Adviser Brent Scowcroft persuaded Bush that a Kurdish victory would lead to the dismemberment of Iraq through the establishment of a separate Kurdish state. Behind this theory lay the pessimistic view that Iraq was unsuited for democracy and that Sunni minority rule through military force was the only formula capable of keeping the country in one piece. The Sunni, or orthodox Muslims, represented less than 40 percent of Iraq's population. But Bush decided he would intervene only if Saddam used fixed-wing aircraft as opposed to helicopters and poison gas against civilians. Otherwise Saddam was free to use whatever equipment he had salvaged from the defeat to suppress the uprisings. The Shiites were crushed and fled to the marshes. The Kurds were crushed and fled to the mountains. The suppression of the uprisings quickly punctured the euphoria of victory. The chief villain of the piece managed to cling to power.

Like Nixon and Kissinger, Bush used the Kurds as a pawn in a geopolitical game. In calling for Saddam's overthrow, Bush evidently had in mind a military coup, a reshuffling of Sunni gangsters in Baghdad rather than the establishment of a freer and more liberal political order. His decision to abandon the Kurds and Shiites has been aptly described by the political commentator William Safire as the turning point of the Bush presidency. "Thanks to the moral cowardice of 26 March," wrote Safire on the first anniversary of the war, "Mr. Bush snatched defeat from the jaws of victory: Saddam remains in power, persecuting his people, and restored Kuwait remains a feudal fiefdom."

During the Gulf crisis America had two major military objectives: to deter the Iraqi forces from continuing their southward march into Saudi Ara-

bia and to roll them out of Kuwait. Operation
Desert Shield achieved the first, and Operation
Desert Storm the second. A neat war, however,
was followed by a messy peace. Few wars in history have achieved their immediate aims so fully
and quickly and yet left behind so much unfinished
business. The war's aftermath was a reminder that
military force, when used to tackle complex political problems, is merely a blunt instrument. The
war also demonstrated that Americans are better
at short, sharp bursts of military intervention designed to restore the status quo than at sustained
political engagement to resolve the underlying ori-
gins of instability in the Middle East. The Gulf war
was Bush's war; he, more than any other individual, deserves credit for the war's achievements and
blame for its shortcomings.

CHAPTER 7

MADRID AND AFTER

According to what is doubtless an apocryphal story, Pope John Paul once declared that two solutions were possible to the Arab-Israeli conflict—the realistic and the miraculous. The realistic would involve divine intervention, the miraculous a voluntary agreement between the parties. A third possible solution, not foreseen by the pope, involves American intervention. The Middle East peace conference that convened in Madrid at the end of October 1991 represented the high-water mark of active American intervention in pursuit of a comprehensive settlement.

Two events of international significance enabled America to revive what it had optimistically come to call the Middle East peace process: the end of the Cold and Gulf wars. The collapse of the Soviet Union as a superpower orphaned Moscow's military clients—Syria, Iraq, Yemen, Libya, and the radical Palestinian factions—and pulled the rug from under the Arab rejectionist front, which always opposed any peace settlement with Israel. Without Soviet arms and diplomatic backing, Arab radicals could do little except sulk in their tents. The Soviet empire's collapse also meant that America no longer had to contend with a credible rival in the Middle East. Soviet-American competition was replaced by Soviet-American cooperation, and America became the dominant power, nearly reducing the Soviet Union to the level of an assistant. Once the Cold War ended, the Middle East naturally ceased to be an arena for superpower conflict. The end of the global contest between the two principal protagonists thus made possible, or at least conceivable, the end of the conflict between the Arabs and the Israelis.

The Gulf war showed the extent to which the ground rules had changed following the Cold War. The scenario that unfolded following Iraq's invasion of Kuwait would have been inconceivable under conditions of intense Soviet-American competitiveness. Iraq's defeat recast inter-Arab relations, dealing a further blow to the rejectionist front. Syria, once the standard-bearer of Arab rejectionism and Moscow's closest Arab ally, joined the American-led coalition against Iraq. The moderate Saudi-Egyptian axis became more powerful and more assertive in pushing for a strong American role. For its Arab members, the hastily assembled alliance with America against the Iraqi dictator now held long-term attractions. The wartime alliance laid the foundation for a peacetime alliance.

Saddam's adventure and the decline of Soviet power also had a profound impact on U.S.-Israeli relations. Together they called into question the notion that Israel was a strategic asset for America. That Israel helped protect American interests against the twin threats of communism and pan-Arab nationalism had in the past justified huge levels of U.S. aid. But the communist threat had vanished, and when the crucial test came in the war with Iraq, America's much vaunted asset proved to be an embarrassment and a liability. By attacking Israel, Saddam tried, but ultimately failed, to achieve two objectives: to turn an Arab-Arab conflict into an Arab-Israeli one and to drive a wedge between the Arabs and America by highlighting America's commitment to Israel. Under the circumstances the best service Israel could offer its ally was to do nothing, to sit back and take punches on the chin. Once Iraqi Scud missiles started falling on Tel Aviv, the Americans were obliged to assume an additional defense burden by rushing in anti-Scud Patriot missile batteries and their crews. Undersecretary of State Lawrence Eagleburger, who had the unenviable task of keeping the Israelis under leash, ended up a virtual hostage in Jerusalem. The most polite word American officials could think of to describe Israel's role was *irrelevant*. Most thought Israel a nuisance and, worse, an expensive nuisance.

American policy makers inevitably questioned whether they needed Israel. What could it offer that America's Arab friends could not provide? The Gulf states were infinitely more valuable as a market for goods and services and as a source of oil. George Bush and James Baker, two former Texas oilmen with no sentimental attachment to Israel, had little difficulty concluding that their country's vital interests lay with the black gold.

The end of the Gulf war gave the Bush administration the opportunity and impetus to reengage in the Arab-Israeli peace process. Saddam Hussein, in one of the curious paradoxes that punctuate Middle East history, could claim some of the credit for the Madrid peace conference. It was he who, in the famous linkage proposal of August 12, 1990, suggested an Israeli withdrawal from all occupied Arab territories as the price for an Iraqi withdrawal from Kuwait.

President Bush rejected the proposed linkage to avoid rewarding Iraqi aggression and to deflate Saddam's claim to be Palestine's champion. But Bush could not, without exposing himself to the charge of double standards, insist that Saddam comply instantly with UN orders to withdraw from Kuwait without acknowledging that Israel should comply with the strikingly similar demands of Security Council Resolution 242, on the table since 1967. Bush's way around this problem was to intimate that he would seek a settlement of the Arab-Israeli dispute once Iraq moved out of Kuwait. Eight trips to the Middle East by Secretary of State Baker, culminating in the crucial Madrid peace conference, showed that the Texas oilmen were as good as their word.

Another reason lay behind President Bush's determination to bring the Arabs and Israelis to the negotiating table: he needed a diplomatic victory to obscure the inconclusive result of the Gulf war and to demonstrate that the crusade against Iraq had been worthwhile despite the casualties, the destruction, the environmental damage, the suffering inflicted on the Iraqi people, and the failure to topple Saddam Hussein. The Gulf war was the jewel in Bush's crown, but it had begun to lose its gleam. Bush's critics at home used Saddam's continued hold on power and Kuwait's and Saudi Arabia's ongoing lack of democracy to tarnish the glow of the Gulf victory. To answer his critics, Bush sought a political achievement of cosmic significance, and that could be found only in an Israeli-Arab solution. Bush was implicitly positing another kind of linkage—one in which victory in the Gulf paved the way to peace in the Middle East.

Getting the Arabs and Israelis to the conference table, however, was no easy matter. Yitzhak Shamir, Israel's right-wing prime minister, was the toughest challenge because his ideological commitment to Greater Israel left little room for compromise. Yet Israel's dependence on American financial help in coping with large-scale Jewish immigration from the Soviet Union gave Bush unprecedented leverage. By withholding the $10 billion loan guarantee requested by Shamir, Bush persuaded the Israelis to participate.

America had given Israel aid totaling $77 billion between 1948 and 1992, and continues to provide an annual subsidy of $3 billion to the Jewish state. Personally, George Bush felt he owed no debt either to Israel or to American Jews. He had been vice president for eight years in the most pro-Israeli administration in American history, yet he got only 5 percent of the Jewish vote in the 1988 presidential election. Bush was thus in a strong position to present Shamir with a choice: keep the occupied territories or keep U.S. support.

President Hafez al-Assad of Syria was another reluctant participant. He ended up accepting the invitation to Madrid not because he suddenly relished the idea of peace with Israel but because he had lost the support of his former superpower patron and had to make his peace with the sole remaining one. To those who accused him of capitulating to American pressure, Assad quoted an Arab adage: "You have to decide whether you want the grapes or a fight with the vineyard keeper." Once Assad agreed to go to Madrid on America's terms, Lebanon meekly followed.

King Hussein of Jordan, having aroused the wrath of America and its Gulf allies by his association with Saddam Hussein, was anxious to rehabilitate himself and resume the receipt of badly needed economic aid. He readily agreed to the formation of a joint Jordanian-Palestinian delegation to provide an umbrella for Palestinian participation in the peace talks.

Excluding the PLO from the peace table was easy: like King Hussein, the PLO had curried disfavor by supporting Saddam during the Gulf crisis. Over the last few years, the political center within the Palestinian national movement had been shifting from the PLO leadership in Tunis to the local leadership in the occupied territories. The *intifada,*

a full-scale Palestinian revolt against Israeli occupation of the West Bank and Gaza that broke out in
December 1987, was initially successful in placing
the Palestinian problem high on the international
agenda but later lost much of its focus and energy
and degenerated into internecine killings. Meanwhile, the Israeli government, led by housing minister Ariel Sharon, accelerated the drive to build
new Jewish settlements on the West Bank. This
made local Arab leaders desperate to play the few
cards they had left before it was too late.

James Baker was blunt with the Palestinians. He
insisted on excluding the PLO and residents of East
Jerusalem, and he demanded a joint Jordanian-
Palestinian delegation rather than an independent
Palestinian one. He refused to make concessions,
even symbolic ones: there would be no Palestinian
flag and no *kaffiyehs,* the traditional Palestinian
headdress. The Palestinians were to turn up in business suits, just like Texas oilmen. In return, Baker
promised the Palestinians substantive negotiations
on an equal footing with Israel—something never
offered before. Concessions from Israel, he argued,
depended on momentum in the peace process.
Once Baker convinced the Palestinians that America's attitude toward Israel had changed, they
agreed to participate on his terms.

During the lead-up to Madrid, Baker followed
the advice of Theodore Roosevelt: Speak softly and
carry a big stick. He also carried a few carrots. And
by skillful manipulation of carrot and stick, he
eventually persuaded all the parties to attend the
conference—his conference.

With Baker as chief puppeteer, the Americans carefully stage-managed the Madrid peace talks. Baker and his aides picked the venue for the conference, issued the formal invitations, provided written assurances to each participant, and laid down the basics for negotiation: Security Council Resolutions 242 and 338 and the principle of exchanging territory for peace.

All the key players but the British appeared in Madrid, although the seeds of the conflict under discussion had been planted in the Balfour Declaration, penned by a Briton. The other notable absentee was the United Nations, whose agenda over the past four and a half decades had been dominated by the Arab-Israeli conflict. Two previous Middle East peace conferences had been held in Switzerland under the auspices of the UN, one in Lausanne in 1949 and the other in Geneva in 1973. The first was a prolonged exercise in futility, the second a one-day fiasco. What these abortive conferences demonstrated was that the world organization was incapable of settling one of the most persistent and dangerous conflicts of modern times. If the peace process launched in Madrid had better prospects of success, it was because of the economic leverage and diplomatic clout of its chief sponsor.

The Soviet Union formally enjoyed the status of a co-sponsor of the Madrid conference, but it was a hollow role. Having been largely passive during the Gulf crisis and war, it was called upon to play junior partner to America in postwar diplomacy. Naming the Soviet Union as a co-sponsor of the conference was helpful to America in two ways.

First, it defended Arab participants from the criticism of their radical constituencies that they were simply marching to an American tune. Second, it provided America with a pliant Soviet partner and a plausible justification for excluding the UN from the action: the Soviet presence legitimized what was in fact a unilateral American diplomatic initiative.

At the opening session in the Palacio Real, President Bush stood as the proud victor in two wars: the Cold War and the Gulf war. He showed magnanimity in victory by saying that the United States and the Soviet Union were there not as rivals but as partners. But President Gorbachev's pathetic speech about his country's economic needs made it obvious that the Soviet Union was there as America's junior partner. The Soviet Union was not in Madrid to compete with America but to compete with Arabs and Israelis for American largess. Gorbachev's speech irrevocably ended any Soviet pretension of independent superpower status.

President Bush was faultlessly evenhanded: by calling for peace based on security he pleased the Israelis; by calling for peace based on fairness he pleased the Palestinians. The United States was simply there to facilitate the search for peace, he said, in one of the few understatements of the conference.

The opening speeches by the heads of the Israeli and Palestinian delegations faithfully reflected the positions of the two sides. Yitzhak Shamir's speech, while long on anti-Arab clichés, was exceedingly short on substance, its tone anachronistic and stale.

He used the platform to deliver the first-ever Israel Bonds speech, an Israeli rallying cry, in front of an Arab audience. His version of the Arab-Israeli conflict was singularly narrow and blinkered, portraying Israel as the victim of Arab aggression and refusing to acknowledge that any evolution had taken place in Arab or Palestinian attitudes. All the Arabs, according to Shamir, wanted to see Israel destroyed; the only difference among them was how to bring about its destruction. By insisting that the root cause of the conflict was not territory but the Arab refusal to recognize the legitimacy of the State of Israel, Shamir came dangerously close to rejecting the basis of the conference—UN Resolutions 242 and 338 and the principle of land for peace.

Haidar Abdul-Shafi, head of the Palestinian delegation, followed Shamir. There was a palpable feeling of history in the making as he read his text in the magnificent Hall of Columns, a sense that this moment would become a benchmark in the quest for reconciliation between Palestinians and Israelis. The soft-spoken doctor from Gaza had one message: that Israeli occupation must end, that the Palestinians had a right to self-determination, and that they were determined to pursue this right until they achieved statehood. The *intifada,* he suggested, had already begun to embody the Palestinian state and to build its institutions and infrastructure. But while staking a claim to Palestinian statehood, Abdul-Shafi qualified it in two significant ways. First, he accepted the need for a transitional stage, provided interim arrangements were not transformed into permanent status. Second, he envisaged a confederation between an ultimately independent Palestine and Jordan. As Abdul-Shafi delivered his speech, Israel's stony-faced prime minister passed a note to a colleague. A joke going around the conference hall was that the note read, "We made a big mistake. We should have let the PLO come."

Abdul-Shafi's speech was both the most eloquent and the most moderate presentation of the Palestinian case made by an official spokesman since the beginning of the conflict. The PLO, despite its growing moderation, had never been able to articulate such a clear-cut peace overture to Israel because of its internal divisions and the constraints of inter-Arab politics. No PLO official had ever been able to declare so unambiguously that a Palestinian state would be ready for a confederation with Jordan. The whole tenor of the speech was more conciliatory and constructive than even the most moderate PLO statements. In the words of one PLO official, Abdul-Shafi's speech was "unreasonably reasonable."

If Yitzhak Shamir found he could no longer rely on the Palestinians to let him off the hook, he had better luck with Syrian foreign minister Farouk al-Sharaa. Sharaa played the old record of rejectionism and vituperation. He was without doubt the most militant and radical Arab representative in Madrid, and he was also the most isolated. The conference degenerated into an exchange of insults between the Israeli and the Syrian. Shamir denounced Syria as one of the world's most repressive and tyrannical regimes. Sharaa replied in kind, denouncing Israel as a terrorist state led by a former terrorist. At a press conference afterward he refused to answer questions from Israeli journalists. Sharaa was like a bat trying to fly in daylight. His performance revealed what a closed, dark place Syria still was, notwithstanding its move from the Soviet into the American camp. Against the background of his strident rejectionism, the Palestinians' readiness for constructive dialogue was all the more striking.

After the plenary session was over, stage two of the peace process began with a series of bilateral meetings between Israel and each of the three Arab delegations. Here too the Syrians were the most intransigent, while the Palestinians seemed more eager than any of the Arab delegations to forge ahead with the talks and to halt Jewish settlement in the occupied territories. As a result of these differences, the common Arab front collapsed. Syria held out for a unified Arab position on its demand of an Israeli commitment to trade the Golan Heights for peace before the bilateral talks began. Among the Palestinian delegates, there was considerable irritation with Syria's attempt to set an overall Arab agenda. They broke ranks with Syria and not only held a meeting with the Israelis but shook hands with them on-camera. What the Palestinians were saying, in effect, was that Syria had no power of veto over Palestine and that they would not allow inter-Arab politics to hold the peace process hostage.

One of the distinguishing marks of the conference was the emergence of a Palestinian-American axis. Of all the delegations, the Palestinian was the only one that agreed to nearly all the American requests on both procedure and substance. The American officials had advised the Palestinians to appeal to the American public, and they followed this advice almost to the neglect of public opinion in other countries. To minimize the risk of an Israeli walkout, the Americans had reviewed several scenarios with the Palestinians before the conference began, and both sides were pleased with the result. In his opening speech, James Baker even paid tribute to Palestinians such as Faisal Husseini and Hanan Ashrawi, leaders of the Palestinian delegation, "whose personal courage in the face of enormous pressures has created the possibility of a better life for Palestinians."

What mattered much more than the polished performance by the Palestinians was that they were a lot closer than the Israelis to the American position in Madrid. They explicitly accepted that the negotiations should be based on UN Resolutions 242 and 338 and the principle of land for peace, whereas Israel did not. They got on board the bus that Baker had warned would come only once, whereas Shamir continued to quibble over the fare, the driver, the rights of other passengers, and the bus's speed, route, and destination.

The official American position toward the Arab-Israeli conflict had remained unchanged since 1967. America supported the exchange of land for peace, refused to acknowledge the Israeli annexation of East Jerusalem, and considered the building of Jewish settlements in the occupied territories illegal and an obstacle to peace. What did change was the evident determination of the Bush administration to do more than repeat these positions like a phonograph record.

In his concluding remarks Baker repeated the polite fiction that America would not impose its ideas but would act as the honest broker in furthering the peace process. But Baker knew, as did everyone else, that resolution of the Arab-Israeli conflict required more than an honest broker. The gulf between the two sides was extremely wide, and America was the only power with the resources and authority to bridge this gulf. In Madrid, America demonstrated that it also has the commitment and determination to pursue its vision of Middle East peace. It was only a beginning, but a fair, and therefore highly promising, beginning.

Subsequent developments soon dashed many of the hopes that the Madrid encounter had raised. Just as the Gulf war was a neat war followed by a messy peace, so Madrid was a neat peace conference with a messy sequel. Kick-starting the peace process was one thing; staying the course was another. In peace as in war the Bush administration proved to be better at generating a concentrated burst of activity than at sustained political and intellectual effort. Once again the Bush administration deserved most of the credit for the promising start and some of the blame for the faltering that followed.

The administration invited the parties to hold bilateral peace talks in Washington starting on December 14, 1991. The Palestinians accepted with alacrity: at long last they would walk the corridors of power. The Israelis, though, delayed their arrival for several days to protest what they saw as an increasingly abrasive and one-sided American approach to the talks. The last thing they wanted was the kind of brisk and concrete down-to-business approach urged by the Americans. Shamir, who had been suspicious of the peace process from the start, came under growing pressure from the settlement lobby and his right-wing coalition partners not to make any concessions on Palestinian autonomy. A past master at playing for time, he resorted to all his familiar tricks of obstinacy, obfuscation, and obstruction.

The issue that Shamir used to spoil the talks was the status of the Palestinians. On the last day of the Madrid talks an understanding was reached specifying that in the bilateral phase the Israelis would negotiate separately with the Palestinians and the Jordanians. Accordingly the Americans prepared two rooms in the State Department, one for the Israeli and Palestinian teams and one for the Israeli and Jordanian teams. But the Israelis underlined their opposition to a separate Palestinian entity by insisting that they negotiate with a joint Jordanian-Palestinian delegation. For two days the heads of the Israeli and Palestinian delegations haggled in the corridor of the State Department, unable to agree even to enter the negotiation room. Their American hosts thoughtfully placed a sofa in the corridor. This bizarre behavior added a new term

to the rich lexicon of the Arab-Israeli conflict—
corridor diplomacy. The only thing the Israeli and
Palestinian negotiators could agree on was that
State Department coffee was undrinkable.

Matters of substance were discussed in the
Israeli-Syrian and the Israeli-Lebanese talks, but
no progress was made. Throughout the talks the
Americans maintained a hands-off approach,
telling the negotiators to sort out their own problems. James Baker was preoccupied with the internal disintegration of the Soviet Union, which
followed the disintegration of its empire in Eastern
Europe. George Bush was preoccupied with domestic problems, not the least of which was his spectacular fall in popularity from its peak during the
Gulf war. The upshot was that the Washington
talks remained bogged down in procedural wran-
gles. Washington represented a step back from
Madrid with no ratchet mechanism and no American intervention to stop the backsliding.

It took another round of D.C. talks, in January
1992, to break the procedural deadlock. The negotiators reached a compromise on the status of the
Palestinians that enabled both sides to claim victory. Israel would negotiate with two separate sub-
committees consisting of nine Palestinians and two
Jordanians on Palestinian-related issues and nine
Jordanians and two Palestinians on Jordanian-
related issues. With a sigh of relief, Hanan Ashrawi, the Palestinian spokeswoman, announced the
end of corridor diplomacy.

The move from corridor diplomacy to a proper

negotiating forum set the alarm bells ringing in Israel. The settlers stepped up their pressure on the government to break off negotiations and crack down harder on *intifada* activity. Shamir's right-wing coalition partners, the Tehia and Moledet parties, resigned because Palestinian autonomy was put on the agenda for future talks. Their resignations deprived Shamir of his majority in the Knesset and forced him to bring forward the date of the elections. With Israel heading for elections in the summer of 1992, the peace process hung in limbo. The prospects for progress looked bleak despite the procedural breakthrough. Throughout the five rounds of bilateral talks that he directed, Shamir seemed intent on scuttling the peace talks and on blaming the Arabs for their failure.

Both Shamir and Bush lost their elections. In June 1992 Yitzhak Rabin, the Labor Party leader, replaced the obdurate Yitzhak Shamir. Replacing Bush after twelve years of Republican rule was President Bill Clinton, who, through his secretary of state, Warren Christopher, promised to continue the Bush administration's policy in the Gulf and to become a more active partner in the Arab-Israeli peace talks.

On assuming power, the Clinton administration gave free rein to its pro-Israeli sympathies. The hallmark of its policy was not active partnership in the peace talks but active partnership with Israel. One of President Clinton's first decisions as president was to grant Israel the $10 billion loan guarantee that his predecessor had made conditional on cooperation in the peace talks. The premise of Clinton's policy seemed to be that Israel could do no wrong, while the Arabs, and especially the Palestinians, could do nothing right.

The Clinton administration's approach to the Middle East was laid out by Martin Indyk, a senior official on the National Security Council, in a May 18, 1993, speech he gave to the pro-Israel Washington Institute for Near East Policy, of which he had been co-founder and executive director. Two elements were listed by Indyk as central: Israel had to be kept strong while the peace process continued, and Iraq and Iran had to be kept weak. Indyk referred to the latter policy as "dual containment":

"Dual containment" derives from an assessment that the current Iraqi and Iranian regimes are both hostile to American interests in the region. Accordingly, we do not accept the argument that we should continue the old balance of power game, building up one to balance the other. . . . We reject it because we do not need it. . . . The coalition that fought Saddam remains together. As long as we are able to maintain our military presence in the region; as long as we succeed in restricting the military ambitions of both Iraq and Iran; and as long as we can rely on our regional allies—Egypt, Israel, Saudi Arabia and the GCC [Gulf Cooperation Council], and Turkey—to preserve the balance of power in our favour in the wider Middle East region, we will have the means to counter both the Iraqi and Iranian regimes.

Dual containment was expected to protect Israel on the eastern front. Regarding the Middle East peace process, Indyk continued, "our approach to the negotiations will involve working with Israel, not against it. We are committed to deepening our strategic partnership with Israel in the pursuit of peace and security." Withdrawing from territory would involve risks to Israel's security, and Israel would undertake these risks only if it knew the United States stood behind it. One way to achieve this would be for America to affirm its commitment to maintaining Israel's military edge. Another would be to establish a partnership to develop and produce high-technology goods such as advanced computers. Real progress in the peace talks, concluded Indyk, would come only with this kind of special relationship between America and Israel.

No similar pledge was made to work with the Arabs. Indyk's speech reflected a shift in American policy, away from the evenhanded approach of the Bush administration and back to the Reagan administration's Israel-first approach. As a result, America in effect abdicated its role as mediator in the peace talks and took the side of one of the protagonists. But the extent of the Clinton administration's one-sidedness was revealed only during the tenth round of talks, which opened in mid-June 1993. In an attempt to move the Israeli-Palestinian talks off dead center, the State Department drafted a paper to serve as the basis for a joint declaration of principles. The Palestinian delegates, however, detected Israel's thumbprints on the paper. Reversing a twenty-six-year-old American policy, the paper endorsed the Israeli claim that East Jerusalem and the rest of the West Bank is disputed rather than occupied territory. The Palestinians rejected the paper even as a starting point for negotiations because it deviated from the terms under which the Madrid peace talks had been initiated. After twenty months and ten rounds, the American-sponsored talks had reached a dead end.

The breakthrough announced in September 1993 was made in Oslo, not Washington. Fifteen sessions of secret talks in Norway over eight months, between two Israeli academicians who were later accompanied by officials and senior PLO officials from Tunis, culminated in an agreement on mutual recognition and on limited Palestinian self-government in Gaza and the West Bank town of Jericho. American ignorance and incompetence in managing the talks helped persuade PLO chairman Yasser Arafat to use the negotiating channel provided by the Norwegians. American officials were left uninformed. Warren Christopher was told of the breakthrough only shortly before it was made public. He and his advisers, who had resisted recognition of the PLO until the last moment, were upstaged. The accord belied the belief that no settlement is possible in the Middle East without external intervention. It also supported Abba Eban's claim that nations are capable of acting rationally when they have exhausted all other alternatives.

Although the Israel-PLO accord was made in Norway, the Declaration of Principles on Palestinian self-government in Gaza and Jericho was signed in Washington, with Bill Clinton acting as master of ceremonies. A handshake between Yitzhak Rabin and Yasser Arafat provided a powerful symbol of the historic reconciliation. Although it was not Clinton who brought together the lugubrious old soldier and the grinning guerrilla fighter, they handed him one of the very few foreign policy successes of his early administration.

President Clinton recognized the need for an American role in supporting the experiment in Palestinian self-government and in keeping the momentum toward comprehensive peace in the Middle East. He repeatedly expressed his determination to use American power and influence to prop up the accord. The economic development of the West Bank and Gaza will require large amounts of money, and the Clinton administration, while reluctant to dip into its own pocket, enthusiastically assumed the role of chief fund-raiser. The idea that America should assemble a global coalition of donors to finance Palestinian self-government was reminiscent of the coalition put together to eject Iraq from Kuwait. "Just as the United States organized a successful international coalition to wage war in the Gulf," proclaimed an uncharacteristically jubilant Warren Christopher, "we will now organize a new coalition—a coalition to breathe life into the Israeli-Palestinian declaration." American deeds, however, did not match these brave words.

In practical terms, American policy boiled down to maintaining Israel's military edge, come what may. President Clinton declared that he would use American power to make sure Israel felt more, not less, secure because of the Oslo accord. Privately he assured Rabin that he had no plans to curtail the annual $3 billion in direct U.S. assistance. He also promised extra funds to finance Israel's withdrawal from Gaza and Jericho and the transfer to Israel of sophisticated military technology, withheld before for security reasons. In contrast, Clinton promised only modest, unspecified "seed money" to the new Palestinian entity.

The document signed in the White House on September 13 was not a fully fledged peace agreement but a declaration of principles accompanied by a detailed timetable that fell a long way short of the Palestinian claim to full independence and statehood. Critical questions such as the rights of the 1948 refugees, the future of Jerusalem, the future of the Jewish settlements in the occupied territories, and the borders of the Palestinian entity were deferred to negotiations at a later stage. Despite all these limitations, the Israel-PLO accord marked a major breakthrough in the century-old conflict between Jews and Arabs over Palestine. What made this accord so significant was that it reconciled the two principal parties in this conflict: Israel and the Palestinians. The purpose of the accord was to bring about a peaceful settlement of the Israeli-Palestinian dispute. Whether or not this objective is achieved, the accord spelled the end of the broader Arab-Israeli conflict. Historically, the neighboring Arab states became involved in this conflict on the side of the Palestinians against the Zionist intruders. Now that the Palestinians themselves had embarked on the road to peace, there was no longer any compelling reason for the Arab states to maintain the state of war against the common enemy. A major pan-Arab taboo had been broken.

The initial reaction of the neighboring Arab states to the Israel-PLO accord was one of suspicion and resentment. Jordan, Syria, and Lebanon were all surprised by Yasser Arafat's solo diplomacy, fearing that he was making a separate deal with Israel, and they were suspicious of Israel's intentions. Arafat defended his decision to sign the accord by presenting it as the first step toward comprehensive peace in the Middle East. There was a general feeling, however, that the PLO chairman had broken rank and, like Anwar Sadat fifteen years earlier, had played into Israel's hands.

The country most directly affected by the Israel-PLO accord was Jordan. The accord posed acute economic, political, constitutional, and security problems for Jordan. As the Jordanian constitutional expert Mustapha Hamarneh explained, "Yasser Arafat did not pull a rabbit out of his hat but a damned camel." In other words, Arafat's Gaza-Jericho deal for the Palestinians involved equally weighty problems for the Jordanians. Traditionally, Jordan and Israel had been tacit allies, joined by a common interest in containing Palestinian nationalism. Now Israel seemed to have changed tack. Jordan feared that Israel might have abandoned its policy of partnership in favor of a new partnership with the PLO. And since roughly half of Jordan's population is Palestinian, Jordan also feared that an influx of Palestinians from the West

Bank to the East Bank would increase the pressure to turn the Hashemite Kingdom of Jordan into the Republic of Palestine. In late September, however, Yitzhak Rabin assured King Hussein at a secret meeting that Israel's pro-Jordanian policy had not changed and that Jordan's interests would be taken into account in Israel's dealings with the PLO.

These assurances encouraged Hussein to proceed with Jordan's general elections as planned. The November 1993 election, the first multiparty election since 1957, yielded what Hussein hoped for: a strengthening of the conservative, the tribal, and the independent blocs and a rebuff to the Islamic Action Front, whose platform opposed the peace talks with Israel. The message for the rest of the region was that Islamic fundamentalists do not necessarily succeed within a democratic framework.

The PLO defection and the Jordanian election results emboldened King Hussein to conduct his own secret talks with the Israeli leaders. On July 25, 1994, the king and Rabin met openly in the White House and, in the presence of a grinning Bill Clinton, pronounced the end of forty-six years of hostility. The Washington Declaration was the closest thing to a peace treaty. Fleshing out the Washington Declaration was a relatively easy task because the king was set on peace at almost any price. Jordan demanded the return of 150 square miles of land occupied by Israel in the Arava Valley, south of the Dead Sea, and a greater share of the water from the Jordan and Yarmuk rivers in the north.

Three more months of bilateral negotiations culminated in the conclusion of a formal peace treaty between Israel and Jordan on October 26. The treaty was signed by Prime Minister Rabin and King Hussein in the baking desert, north of the Red Sea, with President Clinton as their guest of honor. It was the second treaty between Israel and an Arab state in fifteen years and the first one to be signed in the region. The treaty defined the international border between the two countries and committed them to establish full diplomatic relations. It also committed Israel to give high priority to Jordan's special role as the guardian of the Muslim holy shrines in Jerusalem.

In Jordan the treaty was presented as a historic achievement that precludes the possibility of any further eastward expansion by the Zionist movement. But it was Israel's overwhelming power and the atrophy of pan-Arabism that made this treaty possible. King Hussein signed this treaty not simply in order to recover territory and water resources but in order to protect his kingdom against a takeover bid by the Palestinians and in order to forestall the emergence of an Israeli-Palestinian axis. At one stroke, he turned the tables on his Palestinian rival and asserted his own position as Israel's natural ally in the region. With characteristic pragmatism, he adjusted himself to the new reality, in which Israel is the predominant power between Morocco and India.

The king's peace was also dictated by his desire to move closer to America in the post–Cold War era. Nothing was better calculated to please America than a peace treaty with Israel. By taking the plunge and signing such a treaty, the king ensured that Jordan's needs did not go unnoticed in Washington. Following the signing ceremony of the Israel-Jordan peace treaty, Bill Clinton addressed the Jordanian parliament in Amman. He promised that the United States would never let Jordan down, would supply the arms it requires, and would write off its debts, and he even paid homage to the Hashemite dynasty and its services to the Arab cause.

Like the Israel-PLO accord, the Israel-Jordan peace treaty was basically the handiwork of the parties directly concerned. During the negotiations that resulted in the treaty, America surrendered any independent voice and seemed content to play a largely passive role. It embraced Israel's position on most of the core issues and so had little to offer apart from money. Israel concluded a deal in direct talks and largely on her own terms, while America simply facilitated the deal by providing economic incentives to Jordan.

In the case of Israel and Syria, Clinton and Christopher played a rather more active role in trying to bring about a settlement. The political and even cultural gap between these two foes is very deep, and the need for an external mediator is correspondingly greater. President Hafez al-Assad demands the Golan Heights as the price for making peace with Israel. The Golan Heights were lost to Israel in the June 1967 war when Assad was defense minister. He cannot afford to compromise on getting back the entire plateau. The formula he has embraced is "full withdrawal for full peace." He can be flexible over the means—phased withdrawal, demilitarization, Israeli listening posts, even American peacekeepers—but he is utterly inflexible on the principle of full Syrian sovereignty over the Golan Heights.

The negotiations between Israel and Syria continued to proceed at a snail's pace after Labor replaced Likud in power. President Assad insisted not only on total Israeli withdrawal from the Golan Heights but on a comprehensive settlement of the Arab-Israeli conflict. He himself holds the key to a peace settlement between Israel and Lebanon by virtue of his position as the arbiter of Lebanese politics. But he suffered two major setbacks when Arafat and King Hussein concluded separate agreements with Israel. Left in the lurch by his Arab partners, Assad seemed determined to demonstrate, in Henry Kissinger's famous dictum, that "the Arabs cannot make war without Egypt or peace without Syria."

In an effort to steer Syria toward a settlement with Israel, President Clinton held two meetings with Assad while his secretary of state acted as a messenger boy between Damascus and Jerusalem. They were able to offer Assad various economic and political incentives but they were unable to convey an Israeli commitment to full withdrawal from the Golan Heights. In the absence of such a commitment, the gap between Damascus and Jerusalem could be narrowed but it could not be closed. By the end of 1994, the long-awaited breakthrough on the Israeli-Syrian track had failed to materialize. The official line in Damascus was that the status quo was preferable to the terms offered by Israel.

A marked change occurred in America's policy toward the Arab-Israeli conflict following the Democratic victory in the November 1992 presidential elections. The evenhanded approach of the Bush administration was replaced by a feeble Israel-first approach, and the assertive American role in the conduct of peace talks was replaced by a passive style of leadership. America's role, as defined by Clinton, is to help Israel reduce the risks involved in trading territory for peace. This redefinition placed American influence and resources at the service of Israeli diplomacy. It enabled Rabin to break up the Arab front, conclude separate peace agreements with the PLO and Jordan, and isolate Syria. It left the Arabs, and especially the Palestinians, feeling frustrated, disillusioned, and let down by America. The Palestinians, abandoned to Rabin's tender mercies, increasingly doubt that the Oslo accord can lead to genuine autonomy, let alone an independent Palestine. President Assad, who has called for the peace of the brave, confronts an opponent who seems determined to impose the peace of the bully. It is true that Rabin claims that his ultimate goal, like that of the Arabs, is comprehensive peace in the Middle East and that bilateral agreements are the building blocks of such a peace. But for America to offer unconditional support to Israel in all matters relating to Middle East peacemaking is an act of faith rather than an act of statesmanship.

C H A P T E R   8

PAX AMERICANA

One result of Operation Desert Storm, as President Bush proudly observed, was that it enabled America to kick the Vietnam syndrome, to regain self-confidence, to demonstrate that it has both the political will and the military capacity to fight and to win. What Bush did not grasp, or grasped only dimly, is that the war did absolutely nothing to enable the Arabs to kick the post-Ottoman syndrome.

As noted earlier, the post-Ottoman syndrome grew out of the settlement imposed on the region by the European great powers in 1918–22, following the destruction of the Ottoman Empire. Those powers paid little attention to the wishes and aspirations of the local inhabitants. They created states, drew boundaries around them, and appointed their rulers. Some of these changes had no legitimacy in the eyes of the citizens of the new states that were built on the ruins of the Ottoman Empire. Indeed, lack of legitimacy was a basic feature of the new state system. Consequently the postwar settlement created a belt of instability stretching from the Mediterranean to the Persian Gulf. This is the post-Ottoman syndrome, of which Iraq is the most striking example. With a large Kurdish population, a Shiite majority, and Sunni minority rule, Iraq is one of the Middle East's least homogeneous nation-states. It has always been restless and probably always will be. To deal with this restlessness, the Ba'ath regime has habitually resorted to repression at home and aggression abroad. Saddam Hussein pushed these tendencies to their extremes.

Saddam's motives for seizing and declaring Kuwait Iraq's nineteenth province were immediate and economic. He was strapped for cash, so he went for a big bank raid. But the invasion had deeper roots, in the post-Ottoman syndrome. In a sense, Saddam's aggression represented the logical extension of Arab efforts to throw off Western domination, to undo the post-Ottoman divisions. Ironically, the result has been to place this adventure's perpetrators, along with other Arabs, under the kind of Western domination they have been struggling against since Ottoman days.

The war was not simply about Kuwait but about the perpetuation of Western hegemony in the region. By using force to eliminate an independent state, Saddam challenged the old order. If Kuwait had been wiped out, nothing would have stopped the subversion and destruction of the old order. President Bush did not send more than 400,000 American troops to fight for the undemocratic and unloved al-Sabah dynasty but to safeguard Western access to oil and to demonstrate that a sovereign state cannot be snuffed out. By implication he had accepted the old colonial order, with all its anomalies and injustices, as final and inviolate. Changing this order through negotiations was one thing, but changing it by force was unacceptable. The war was thus an affirmation of a fundamental principle of international law—namely, the inadmissibility of acquiring territory by force—a principle, incidentally, at the heart of UN resolutions for resolving the Arab-Israeli dispute.

In the process of upholding international law, America vastly increased its power in the region. The result of the Gulf war was thus the reverse of what Saddam intended. By seizing Kuwait, he wanted to assert Iraq's mastery over the Persian Gulf and to strike a blow at America's position there, including its influence over oil prices. The war, however, shattered Iraq, and America emerged as the region's unchallenged power. It became, in fact, as dominant after the Gulf war as Britain had been after World War I. If the period between the world wars was, as the Middle East specialist Elizabeth Monroe has phrased it, "Britain's moment in the Middle East," the Gulf war marked the beginning of America's moment in the Middle East. Pax Britannica was succeeded, after a long and turbulent period of Arab self-assertion, by Pax Americana.

Bush couched his call to war not in materialistic

but in idealistic terms. To mobilize domestic support, he invested the war with a higher moral purpose. Woodrow Wilson took America into World War I and Franklin D. Roosevelt took it into World War II by appealing to America's idealism. George Bush, consciously or unconsciously, followed their example. On January 16, 1991, he stated that launching military action against Iraq would make possible a "New World Order, a world where the rule of law, not the law of the jungle, governs the conduct of nations." While working to restore the old order, he invested it with the clothes of the new.

Although the New World Order was a recurrent theme during the Gulf crisis, it consisted of more rhetoric than substance. Its purpose was to drum up domestic support for the war and to provide a rallying cry for the international coalition led by the United States, and this purpose was well served. On closer examination, however, the New World Order was hardly distinguishable from the old. It was based on the status quo, on existing states and existing frontiers. Its keystone, like that of the old, was stability. The new order, like the old, recognized only state rights, not individual or group rights, especially if these were liable to disturb international stability. In no sense was the New World Order a crusade to launch a democratic revolution around the world. Oppressed minorities like the Kurds and irredentist groups like the Shiites received no support from America in their struggle for political reform.

The New World Order was essentially a cloak

for covering American hegemony in the international system. Perhaps it was inevitable that the criteria used to determine the new order would be the same as those used after World War I: the interests of the victors. This is why the New World Order evoked almost as much suspicion and hostility among the people of the Middle East as the war that preceded it. King Hussein expressed these sentiments with particular vehemence when he claimed that "the real purpose behind this destructive war, as proven by its scope . . . is to destroy Iraq and rearrange the area in a manner far more dangerous to our nation's present and future than the Sykes-Picot Agreement." The reference to the secret agreement of 1916, which ignored Arab nationalist aspirations and divided the spoils of war between Britain and France, was revealing. In Arab eyes Sykes-Picot is the enduring symbol of Western perfidy and selfishness. Given the Arab view of the Gulf war depicted by King Hussein, it was predictable that Arabs would be similarly disturbed by the postwar settlement.

The Third World also saw the war as a Western crusade against the Arabs. Few accepted the claim that it was launched in disinterested pursuit of collective security, and many resented what they viewed as America's manipulation of the United Nations to legitimize a highly dubious enterprise. Some Third World UN representatives felt the Gulf war proved only that America could move into a trouble spot with fancy technology, smash up the place, leave all the existing political problems unsolved while creating new ones, and then go home to celebrate victory. Even those who conceded that the war was justified were critical of America for leaving Iraq to fester and for failing to deliver on its promises of a better future.

What the New World Order amounts to is the old order minus the Soviet Union. There is no New World Order but a new world balance. The collapse of the Soviet Union left America the sole, undisputed superpower. During the Gulf crisis, America enjoyed greater freedom to act and to exercise international leadership than at any time since 1945. In previous Middle East crises, America had to contend with Soviet rivalry and run the risk that a local war would escalate into a superpower confrontation. During the Gulf crisis, the Soviets meekly followed the American lead. America used this unprecedented freedom to reverse Saddam's aggression but not to bring about his downfall.

Does Saddam's survival mean the Gulf war failed, and does it make a mockery of the American claim to a New World Order? Critics of the Bush administration thought that it did. Defenders retorted that the war attained all its objectives and had to be considered an unqualified success: Kuwait was liberated, Saddam was defeated and discredited, and everybody in the region knew it. The war certainly confirmed America's ability to deal with troublemakers and defend its vital interests in the Middle East. America also commanded more diplomatic leverage, more political clout, and better strategic facilities than at any previous phase of its Middle East involvement. These continue to be the props of Pax Americana. Yet America's capacity to change the political landscape of the Middle East was considerably more limited in the twilight of the Bush administration than it had been in the first flush of victory. By halting the Gulf offensive prematurely, Bush seriously impaired his own and his successor's ability to set the agenda for postwar reconstruction. By standing aside and permitting Saddam to crush the Kurdish and Shiite uprisings, Bush helped ensure the triumph of the old order in Iraq.

Following the hostilities, the Bush administration came up with a five-point plan for the future of the Middle East. The elements of this plan, the "five pillars of wisdom," as one foreign policy expert dubbed them, were democracy, economic development, arms control, Gulf security, and a settlement of the Arab-Israeli conflict. It was a sound and well-thought-out plan that sought to avert repetition of past mistakes. But the plan was never put into practice. As so often in the past, American leaders, whose attention span is notoriously short, did not stay the course. Consequently the moral credit they won by liberating Kuwait was quickly dissipated, and the opportunity to make a fresh start frittered away.

Only one item on the Bush administration's postwar agenda received serious and sustained attention: the Palestinian problem, which previous Republican administrations had tried to keep on the back burner to concentrate on America's economic interests in the Persian Gulf. But the two problems could not be kept apart, because Arabs tended to judge America by its position on the Palestinian problem. During the Gulf crisis, Arabs commonly accused America of double standards, of insisting on swift and unconditional Iraqi withdrawal from Kuwait while condoning Israel's continuing occupation of Arab lands. Saddam would not have been able to manipulate the Palestinian issue to his advantage had its resolution not been so important to Arabs everywhere and such a salient issue in inter-Arab politics.

America rejected Saddam's version of linkage between the Gulf and Arab-Israeli conflicts but it did promise to seek a solution to the Palestinian problem after resolving the Kuwait problem. Although the promise to promote an Arab-Israeli settlement was not new, this time words were followed by deeds. The chief flaw in the approach of previous administrations was that, while offering to act as an honest broker, they provided Israel with open-ended economic, diplomatic, and military assistance, enabling it to defy the will of the international community.

In 1991 James Baker's tireless diplomacy, coupled with President Bush's economic pressure on Israel, indicated a fundamental change. The Israel-first approach gave way to an evenhanded approach. Had Bush not forced Israel to choose between U.S. aid and West Bank settlements, Yitzhak Shamir might have won the 1992 elections and the peace process might have continued to wither. Under the Bush-Baker team, America revived the peace process by defeating communism in the Cold War, Arab radicalism in the Gulf war, and Israeli expansionism in the war over the loan guarantees.

But President Clinton abruptly reverted to a robust Israel-first approach reminiscent of the Reagan years. In the Persian Gulf, the new administration adopted a policy of dual containment, of keeping both Iran and Iraq weak, isolated, under pressure from opposition forces at home, and cut off from the world economic and trading system. While dual containment is an improvement on America's traditional policy of playing Iran and Iraq against each other, it is a negative strategy requiring relentless effort to deny the two nations access to the international capital and arms markets and to curb their capacity for mischief making. It does not address the underlying problems of regional unrest, such as the denial of democracy and human rights by authoritarian regimes and the gap between rich and poor. It ties America to an inherently unstable status quo in the Persian Gulf.

The change of administration led to an even more striking discontinuity in the Arab-Israeli peace talks. Whereas the Bush administration was the manager and the driving force behind the Madrid peace process, the Clinton administration adopted a low-key, hands-off approach. President Clinton's attitude toward the use of force by Israel—the deportation of the Hamas activists in December 1992 and the bombing of Lebanon in July 1993—was extraordinarily indulgent. He also tolerated the use of American aid for large-scale housing projects on the West Bank under the Labor government. Toward the PLO Clinton remained consistently hostile until Israel's sudden recognition of the organization just before signing the Oslo accord forced his hand.

The secret talks between Israel and the PLO not only produced a separate deal but also buried the American-made formula for resolving the Arab-Israeli conflict. King Hussein's treaty with Israel was not part of the Middle East peace process but a unilateral move to protect his own position. Instead of providing leadership in the search for a fair and comprehensive settlement, the Clinton administration helped Israel to impose its own terms on the Palestinians and the Jordanians.

Of the two agreements, the one between Israel and the PLO is considerably more important, because it touches the core of the Arab-Israeli conflict. America pledged its support for the experiment in Palestinian self-government but, measured in financial terms, its contribution has been derisory. Economic conditions in Gaza and the West Bank actually deteriorated in the year following the inauguration of Palestinian self-rule. Nor was there any visible progress toward democracy to compensate for the poverty and material deprivation that the opulation had to endure.

Consequently, popular support for the deal that Yasser Arafat had struck with Israel began to decline, and opposition groups, both secular and religious, stepped up their attacks on the peace talks. The most significant of these groups is Hamas, the Islamic resistance movement, which had been opposed to negotiations with the Jewish state from the start. Hamas's ultimate goal is an Islamic state over the whole of Palestine. As the negotiations on Palestinian self-government lurched from one crisis to the next, Hamas steadily gained ground in Gaza and the West Bank at the expense of the PLO. Meanwhile, the military wing of Hamas mounted a series of attacks on Israeli civilians and soldiers, partly in retaliation for atrocities committed by militant Israeli settlers and partly in an attempt to derail the peace talks.

To help keep the peace talks on track, America has to step up its moral and material support for the forces of moderation on the Palestinian side. America also needs to become more engaged, to commit resources on a much bigger scale and to spread them more evenly if it is to succeed in forging a comprehensive peace settlement in the Middle East on the anvil of the Israel-PLO accord. America has the right and the obligation to promote such a settlement, because if it does not, no one else will. In the absence of a comprehensive settlement, the entire Middle East, Israel included, will be condemned to perpetual strife, violence, and bloodshed.

As Israel's supporters in Washington never tire of pointing out, a settlement of the Arab-Israeli dispute will not be a panacea for the region's ills. Civil wars and interstate conflicts have plenty of other sources, some going back to the order imposed by the victors after World War I. There are also social, economic, religious, and ethnic tensions that have little or nothing to do with the legacy of colonial domination or the century-old conflict between Jews and Arabs in Palestine.

The Bush administration's program for reconstruction after the Gulf war pinpointed some of the region's most serious problems: the authoritarian nature of most Arab regimes, economic underdevelopment, the arms race, and the absence of a viable framework for Gulf security. Solving the Arab-Israeli dispute will not give America a magic wand for eliminating these evils. But it will ease tensions, remove a major Arab grievance against the West, and make the area's residual problems easier to address.

Instability is endemic in the Middle East, and nothing will eradicate it. The 1993 accord cannot ensure a new era of harmony and brotherhood, but that is no reason for America to relax its efforts. On the contrary, lack of progress in achieving the wider agenda only underscores the need to redouble American efforts to achieve a decisive breakthrough on the Arab-Israeli front.

Much has been written in recent years about the Islamic threat to Western interests in the Middle East. It is fashionable, but also simplistic, to suggest that the threat posed by Islamic fundamentalism has replaced the Soviet threat. For those who need an enemy to combat, militant Islam is a convenient bugbear replacing the Soviet bear. Moreover, in the battle against the Islamic threat, some argue, Israel is a natural ally to the West, just as it had been during the Cold War. This argument is used to revive the view of Israel as a strategic asset, a view called into question by the experience of the Gulf war.

A subtler version of the obsession with the Islamic threat appears in an article titled "Clash of Civilizations?" by Samuel P. Huntington, a Harvard University professor of government. Huntington maintains that the primary source of conflict in the post–Cold War world is not economic or ideological but cultural. The wars of kings were replaced in the eighteenth and nineteenth centuries by wars of nations, then by wars of ideologies, and now by wars of civilizations. "The clash of civilizations will dominate world politics," Huntington writes. "The fault lines between civilizations will be the battle lines of the future." The next world war, he implies, will be between Islamic civilization and the West or between Confucian Asian civilization and the West.

The Gulf war, argues Huntington, provided a foretaste of this battle. But it did nothing of the sort. It is true that Saddam Hussein and his supporters attempted to present the Gulf war as a clash between civilizations, between the West and Islam, but only the gullible will accept this interpretation. The Gulf war was a traditional interstate war in which the participants were prompted by traditional state interests. Saddam invaded Kuwait for Persian Gulf oil, and most of the region's Muslim states joined the Western allies in the campaign to turn him back. The Arab and Muslim worlds had few illusions about Saddam or the campaign to thwart him. As Fouad Ajami, a leading expert on the Middle East, has observed,

The fight in the Gulf was seen for what it was: a bid for primacy met by an imperial expedition that laid it to waste. A circle was closed in the Gulf: where once the order in the region "east of Suez" had been the work of the British, it was now provided by Pax Americana. The new power standing sentry in the Gulf belong to the civilization of the West, as did the prior one. But the American presence had the anxious consent of the Arab lands of the Persian Gulf.

Having checked Saddam and having expanded so spectacularly its influence, America is uniquely placed to promote a new political dynamic in the Middle East. Instead of seeking new enemies and threats to combat, it should help its friends, old and new, address the real problems of the Middle East. If Syria and Lebanon make peace with Israel, most of the remaining Arab states will follow. Militant Islamic movements, which thrive on the conflict with the Jewish state, would then lose much of their appeal. The renegade regimes of Iraq and Libya would be encircled and Iran's capacity for causing mischief largely neutralized. Above all, an important basis of Arab authoritarianism would disappear. For nearly half a century the conflict with Israel has been used by soldiers and strongmen to capture and retain power. Israel, on the other hand, likes to present itself as a "light unto the nations," a shining example of democracy in a sea of authoritarianism. The wise course for America is not to bolster Israel as a strategic partner in an unwinnable war against an imaginary Islamic threat but to encourage Israel to contribute to stability, democracy, and economic development throughout the region.

A relative newcomer to the Middle East, America has failed to develop a coherent strategy for dealing with this vital but volatile region. Most of America's mistakes in the last half century can be traced to the combination of globalism and the Israel-first approach. Now that the Cold War is over, there is a powerful case for abandoning the globalist perspective in favor of a more constructive, problem-solving regionalist approach. Equally powerful is the case for abandoning the Israel-first approach in favor of a more even-handed approach in working for a settlement of the Arab-Israeli conflict. And now that America is the unrivaled superpower in the Middle East, the time has also finally come to address the other major problems of the region, the problems associated with the post-Ottoman syndrome.

NOTES ON SOURCES

Introduction

4 " 'the most penetrated . . . world' ": L. Carl Brown, *International Politics and the Middle East: Old Rules, Dangerous Games* (Princeton: Princeton University Press, 1984), p. 4.

5 " 'the history . . . others' ": M. E. Yapp, *The Near East Since the First World War* (London and New York: Longman, 1991), p. 3.

5 " 'the dominant . . . powers' ": Ibid., p. 438.

Chapter 1: The Post-Ottoman Syndrome

13 "As observed by '. . . Iraqi politics' ": Elie Kedourie, *England and the Middle East: The Destruction of the Ottoman Empire, 1914–1921* (London: Bowes and Bowes, 1956), pp. 212–13.

14 " 'Iraq was created . . . and the Shiites' ": Quoted in Pierre Salinger with Erik Laurent, *Secret Dossier: The Hidden Agenda Behind the Gulf War* (London: Penguin Books, 1991), p. 14.

15 " 'In short . . . intended to violate' ": Quoted in Michael L. Dockrill and Douglas J. Goold, *Peace Without Promise: Britain and the Peace Conferences, 1919–1923* (London: Batsford, 1981), pp. 163–64.

18 " 'a peace to end all peace' ": David Fromkin, *A Peace to End All Peace: Creating the Modern Middle East, 1914–1922* (London: Penguin Books, 1989), p. 5.

18 Elizabeth Monroe, *Britain's Moment in the Middle East, 1914–1971* (London: Chatto and Windus, 1981).

22 "Declining support . . . ever since": Avi Shlaim, *The Politics of Partition: King Abdullah, the Zionists, and Palestine, 1921–1951* (New York: Columbia University Press, 1990; Oxford: Oxford University Press, 1990).

24 " 'It seemed . . . the Arab world' ": Nahum Goldmann, *The Autobiography of Nahum Goldmann: Sixty Years of Jewish Life* (New York: Holt, Rinehart and Winston, 1969), pp. 289–90.

26 "Palestine has become . . . 1917": Anthony Parsons, *They Say the Lion: Britain's Legacy to the Arabs—A Personal Memoir* (London: Jonathan Cape, 1986), pp. 149–50.

Chapter 2: Succeeding John Bull

27 " 'too damned much . . . abroad' ": Wm. Roger Louis, *The British Empire in the Middle East, 1945–1951: Arab Nationalism, the United States and Postwar Imperialism* (Oxford: Clarendon Press, 1984), p. 45.

29 " 'have his hand . . . windpipe' ": Keith Kyle, *Suez* (London: Weidenfeld and Nicolson, 1991), p. 136.

29 " 'It . . . Anglo-American alliance' ": Ibid.

30 " 'the lion's last roar' ": Chester L. Cooper, *The Lion's Last Roar: Suez, 1956* (New York: Harper & Row, 1978).

Chapter 3: America Between Arabs and Israelis

39 " 'The simple truth . . . with Israel' ": Jimmy Carter, *The Blood of Abraham* (Boston: Houghton Mifflin, 1985), p. 54.

39 On globalists and regionalists: Malcolm H. Kerr, *America's Middle East Policy: Kissinger, Carter and the Future*, IPS Papers, No. 14 (Beirut: Institute for Palestine Studies, 1980), pp. 8–11.

48–49 " 'amounted to . . . for accepting it' ": George Ball, "The Coming Crisis in Israeli-American Relations," *Foreign Affairs* 58, no. 2 (Winter 1979–80).

51 " 'Sadat was not . . . Sinai agreement' ": Jimmy Carter, *Keeping Faith: Memoirs of a President* (New York: Bantam, 1982), pp. 396–97.

Chapter 4: Realpolitik in the Gulf

64 " 'Documents . . . continue fighting' ": Christopher Hitchens, "Why We Are Stuck in the Sand," *Harper's Magazine*, January 1991.

68 " 'wooed, won . . . America' ": R. K. Ramazani, "Who Lost America? The Case of Iran," *Middle East Journal* 36, no. 1 (Winter 1982).

68 "At first Carter . . . inimical to Islam": Roy Mottahedeh, *The Mantle of the Prophet: Religion and Politics in Iran* (New York: Penguin Books, 1987), pp. 190–91.

70 " 'Let our position . . . military force' ": State of the Union address, January 23, 1980. Text in *The New York Times*, January 24, 1980.

71 "Some liberal critics . . . on Iran": Hitchens, op. cit.

Chapter 5: Tilting Toward Iraq

Stephen J. R. Cass, "Taking Sides: U.S. Policy Towards Iraq During the Iran-Iraq War," Ph.D. dissertation, Oxford University, 1994. I have drawn heavily and with gratitude in this chapter on the work of Mr. Cass, an American student who wrote his doctoral thesis under my supervision.

73 Gary Sick, *October Surprise: America's Hostages in Iran and the Election of Ronald Reagan* (New York: Times Books, 1991).

75 "Although a *New York Times* inquiry . . . Washington's permission": Seymour M. Hersh, "U.S. Cleared Iran Arms Sales," *International Herald Tribune*, December 9, 1991.

76 "Yet the Reagan administration's . . . Arab states": Eric Hooglund, "The Policy of the Reagan Administration Toward Iran," in Nikki R. Keddie and Mark J. Gasiorowski, eds., *Neither East Nor West: Iran, the Soviet Union, and the United States* (New Haven: Yale University Press, 1990), p. 181.

78 " 'Our principle . . . is threatened' ": Barry Rubin, "The United States and the Middle East," in Robert O. Freedman, ed., *The Middle East After the Israeli Invasion of Lebanon* (Syracuse: Syracuse University Press, 1986), p. 84.

80 " 'to prevent . . . area' ": Robert C. McFarlane, "A Crusade Stalled, a Risk Averted," *Los Angeles Times*, July 27, 1988.

83 On Kuwaiti manipulation of the United States: Theodore Draper, "American Hubris: From Truman to the Persian Gulf," *The New York Review of Books*, July 16, 1987.

84 "The sequence of events . . . American naval escorts": Daniel Yergin, *The Prize: The Epic Quest for Oil, Money and Power* (New York: Simon and Schuster, 1991), p. 765.

84 "It would not go 'halvies' with the Russians": Quoted in Yergin, *The Prize*, p. 765.

85 " 'imposing their will . . . neutral shipping' ": *The New York Times*, June 8, 1987.

86 " 'what is driving . . . lifeline' ": *The Washington Post*, May 31, 1987.

87 " 'Reagan's junta' ": Theodore Draper, "Reagan's Junta," *The New York Review of Books*, January 29, 1987.

Chapter 6: Desert Shield and Desert Storm

90 "In January 1990 . . . the Export-Import Bank": Don Oberdorfer, *The Washington Post Magazine*, March 17, 1991.

91 " 'In a playground . . . on his side' ": John Merritt, "UK Envoys Turned Blind Eye," *The Observer*, July 28, 1991.

91 " 'by God . . . half of Israel' ": *Baghdad Domestic Service*, April 2, 1990. Quoted in Efraim Karsh and Inari Rautsi, *Saddam Hussein: A Political Biography* (London: Brassey's, 1991), p. 210.

93 " 'We have no opinion . . . Kuwait' ": Quoted in Pierre Salinger with Eric Laurent, *Secret Dossier: The Hidden Agenda Behind the Gulf War* (London: Penguin Books, 1991), p. 58.

96 " 'We're not discussing intervention' ": Bob Woodward, *The Commanders* (New York: Simon and Schuster, 1991), p. 225.

96 " 'This is no time to go wobbly, George' ": American television program called "The Washington Version."

96 " 'naked aggression' ": Woodward, *The Commanders*, p. 234.

97 " 'The mission . . . defensive' ": Ibid., p. 277.

98 "The Jordanian king . . . dialogue": *White Paper: Jordan and the Gulf Crisis, August 1990–March 1991* (The Government of the Hashemite Kingdom of Jordan, Amman, August 1991).

99 " 'I have not . . . Rubicon' ": Woodward, *The Commanders*, p. 326.

100 " 'go the extra . . . peace' ": Ibid., p. 335.

102 " 'Thanks to the . . . fiefdom' ": William Safire, "The Iraqi Isn't Out of Trouble," *International Herald Tribune*, January 14, 1992.

Chapter 7: Madrid and After

114 " 'We made a big mistake . . . the PLO come' ": Thomas L. Friedman, "Lots of Posturing—and a Little Hope," *International Herald Tribune*, November 4, 1991.

114 " 'unreasonably reasonable' ": Afif Safieh, the PLO representative in London.

116 " 'whose personal . . . Palestinians' ": Middle East Peace Conference at the Royal Palace, Madrid, November 1, 1991.

121–22 " 'Dual containment' derives from . . . Iranian regimes' ": John Law, "Martin Indyk Lays Out the Clinton Approach," *Middle East International* 452 (June 11, 1993).

124 " 'Just as . . . declaration' ": Quoted in Muhammad Hallaj, "Can the US Run the Peace?" *Middle East International* 459 (September 24, 1993).

126 " 'Yasser Arafat . . . camel' ": Quoted in Nora Boustany, "King Hussein Fears Prospects for Peace Could Raise Premature Hopes in Jordan," *International Herald Tribune*, September 18–19, 1993.

Chapter 8: Pax Americana

136 " 'the real purpose behind this . . . Agreement' ": Address to the nation by King Hussein, Amman, February 6, 1991. *White Paper: Jordan and the Gulf Crisis, August 1990–March 1991* (The Government of the Hashemite Kingdom of Jordan, Amman, August 1991), p. 62.

138 " 'five pillars of wisdom' ": Expression heard from Geoffrey Kemp at a conference.

144 " 'The clash . . . future' ": Samuel P. Huntington, "A Clash of Civilizations?" *Foreign Affairs* 72, no. 3 (Summer 1993).

144 " 'The fight . . . Gulf' ": Fouad Ajami, "The Summoning," *Foreign Affairs* 72, no. 4 (September–October 1993).

FOR THE BEST IN PAPERBACKS, LOOK FOR THE

In every corner of the world, on every subject under the sun, Penguin represents quality and variety—the very best in publishing today.

For complete information about books available from Penguin—including Puffins, Penguin Classics, and Arkana—and how to order them, write to us at the appropriate address below. Please note that for copyright reasons the selection of books varies from country to country.

In the United Kingdom: Please write to *Dept. JC, Penguin Books Ltd, FREEPOST, West Drayton, Middlesex UB7 0BR.*

If you have any difficulty in obtaining a title, please send your order with the correct money, plus ten percent for postage and packaging, to *P.O. Box No. 11, West Drayton, Middlesex UB7 0BR*

In the United States: Please write to *Consumer Sales, Penguin USA, P.O. Box 999, Dept. 17109, Bergenfield, New Jersey 07621-0120.* VISA and MasterCard holders call 1-800-253-6476 to order all Penguin titles

In Canada: Please write to *Penguin Books Canada Ltd, 10 Alcorn Avenue, Suite 300, Toronto, Ontario M4V 3B2*

In Australia: Please write to *Penguin Books Australia Ltd, P.O. Box 257, Ringwood, Victoria 3134*

In New Zealand: Please write to *Penguin Books (NZ) Ltd, Private Bag 102902, North Shore Mail Centre, Auckland 10*

In India: Please write to *Penguin Books India Pvt Ltd, 706 Eros Apartments, 56 Nehru Place, New Delhi 110 019*

In the Netherlands: Please write to *Penguin Books Netherlands bv, Postbus 3507, NL-1001 AH Amsterdam*

In Germany: Please write to *Penguin Books Deutschland GmbH, Metzlerstrasse 26, 60594 Frankfurt am Main*

In Spain: Please write to *Penguin Books S. A., Bravo Murillo 19, 1° B, 28015 Madrid*

In Italy: Please write to *Penguin Italia s.r.l., Via Felice Casati 20, I-20124 Milano*

In France: Please write to *Penguin France S. A., 17 rue Lejeune, F-31000 Toulouse*

In Japan: Please write to *Penguin Books Japan, Ishikiribashi Building, 2-5-4, Suido, Bunkyo-ku, Tokyo 112*

In Greece: Please write to *Penguin Hellas Ltd, Dimocritou 3, GR-106 71 Athens*

In South Africa: Please write to *Longman Penguin Southern Africa (Pty) Ltd, Private Bag X08, Bertsham 2013*